Second Thoughts
Further Adventures
in the French Trade

Second Thoughts
Further Adventures in the French Trade

by Jeffrey Mehlman

New York:
The Unconscious in Translation

The Unconscious in Translation is grateful for the subvention awarded by the Boston University Center for the Humanities which helped to make publication of this book possible.

ISBN 978-1-942254-17-1

TABLE OF CONTENTS

For Alicia

for Natalia and Ezra

1

Second Thoughts:
Further Adventures in the French Trade

The density of a life or text can arguably be calibrated in terms of a specific relation between contiguity (which the linguist Roman Jakobson called metonymy) and repetition (or metaphor). One begins with the expectation of a linear advance and ends up with something of a rediscovery of what one assumed one had left behind. In my own case the thought was brought home by the circumstance in which I first sought to set down these introductory pages of what may be characterized as a second volume of adventures in the French trade. I was waiting for the outpatient surgery known as blepharoplasty, a winnowing away of the accumulated flesh weighing down eyelids, forcing them to droop. The most common intention of such surgery is aesthetic, its mode being elective, and thus the target of an irony that may be imagined. In recent years, however, the much reviled bureaucracy of the American insurance industry has determined that there is a purely functional basis for performing the operation in question. The weighted down eyelid in many a case, including my own, might be deemed an obstacle to one's range or field of vision, and—for a professional reader such as myself—a certifiable impediment to the performance of one's professional duty. Whence the elaboration of the category of an insurable blepharoplasty, an instance that rendered my disadvantage available to remedy at a less than ruinous cost.

Now all this might be only minimally or incidentally related to my life as a (writing) reader, or at least so it might seem, were it not that I suddenly recognized a motif out of the preface of my *first* volume of *Adventures in the French Trade*. For the preface of that volume saw me similarly awaiting a minor operation to be performed a day later in a Boston hospital. That operation entailed the use of a green light laser to vaporize the excess tissue of an organ that, I wrote, had become so much the area of expertise of the physician brother of a famous novelist that it was long referred to in certain French circles as the "proustate."[1] (In the years since the publication of that first volume, the Web has made access to the complete text of Proust's *La Prostatectomie dans l'hypertrophie de la prostate* a very few keys on the computer away.) So the "end games" of the current volume share with its predecessor not only an inception in an experience of minor surgery, but an excision of what was called "excess tissue" in a first volume and "accumulated flesh" in its successor. Linear advance gives way to the oddest of repetitions.

A further point of intersection between this opening of what might be construed as a second volume in a series and the first chapter of its predecessor is afforded by an apparent coincidence affecting the term "brother." My own elder brother's involuntary activation of what had begun to be called a negative RH factor in the blood of his—that is, our—mother, she who was ignorant of French but first-named "Frances," with its potentially catastrophic consequences for me (and that, apparently, from the time of his birth on the day in June 1940 that the Germans began their occupation of Paris) just happens to involve the relation of brotherhood (as in Proust's brother) in its relation with the operation—a massive transfusion—that saved my life.

Now the eyelid of my recent operation just happens to figure the node of an associative network in a speculative essay by the French novelist Pascal Quignard. It is titled *La haine de la musique.*[2] The novelist's argument zeroes in on the utter passivity of the ear in music in relation to the painter's eye. "Ears, where are thy eyelids?," as Quignard puts it. The absence, in the case of music, of an acoustical equivalent in sound of the defensive shield or eyelid protecting the ego from what it prefers not to see makes of music the very model of the unconscious. And that circumstance, as though drawing on my own minor

---

1 *Adventures in the French Trade: Fragments Toward a Life* (Stanford University Press, 2010), p. XIV.
2 Pascal Quignard, *La Haine de la musique* (Paris: Gallimard, 1997).

instances of surgery, eyelid and prostate, doubles its aforementioned query with a second one: "Ears, where is thy foreskin?"[3] The excess tissue of the enlarged prostate and the accumulated flesh of the eyelid are joined in their combined resistance to—or filtering of—the music of the unconscious, the unconscious as music.

Now all this structures to an extent the first volume of "adventures" in that music ends up a constant of the analyses offered in that book, but one which is consistently resisted in its association with my brother. Here the key text turns out to be the consideration of the career of Charles Munch, the masterful conductor of the Boston Symphony, but one whose star status in America right after World War II followed directly upon his career as a star of the cultural scene of Nazi-occupied Paris. And my experience of Munch, however sublime, was linked with the service of my brother, a talented musician, gifted with perfect pitch, as a member of the Tanglewood Festival chorus.

The chapter on Munch and his star billing as conductor of the Société des Concerts du Conservatoire de Paris during the years of the Second World War attended as well to his championing of the work of a forgotten composer, Alfred Bachelet, who was honorary president of the wartime musical section of the Groupe Collaboration. More specifically, I spoke of Munch's performance of the premiere of Bachelet's government-commissioned symphonic cantata of 1942, titled "Sûryâ."[4] It was a setting of a poem by Leconte de Lisle in praise of "pure blooded races" and the solar "warrior" ensuring the peaceful existence of men of those races. In brief, it was a piece of Vichy propaganda, which just happened to be paired with a choral concert version of the Grail music from *Lohengrin*, in arrangements first presented in 1936 at Bayreuth under Furt-wängler's direction. Bachelet's "Sûryâ," that is, is readable as occupied France's sympathetic wartime response to Wagner.

Now the opposition between Wagner and the French, which is a figuration of an opposition between music and poetry, has its *locus classicus* in a Mallarmé text of 1885, "Richard Wagner, rêverie d'un poëte français." It happens as well to have been the focus of my senior dissertation as a Harvard undergraduate in 1965. But perhaps the best access we have to the Wagner/Mallarmé (or music/poetry) question is to be found in Mallarmé's poem

---

3 Ibid., p. 110.
4 *Adventures*, p. 27.

of tribute to Wagner, published in 1886 under the title "Hommage" in *La Revue wagnérienne*. The poem pits an abandoned temple, replete with furniture (*mobilier*) draped, apparently for storage, in fabric of rippled silk (*moire*), and its principal pillar (*pilier*), on the one hand, against trumpets of swooning gold (*or pâmé*), emblem of the "god Richard Wagner," celebrating his rite poorly silenced (*mal tu*) by sobs (*sanglots*) of ink. On the one hand, that is, the white-covered *moire* of the over-upholstered furniture and "principal pillar" of what may be the archaic and overly explicit (or overstuffed) theatre of Victor Hugo (who happened to have died on a May 22, which was Wagner's birthday) or the maximalist music drama of Wagner; and, on the other, the poorly or incompletely silenced rite trumpeted by Wagner in the swooning gold of a new aesthetic dispensation.

Now for all the apparent randomness of the Mallarmé poem just sketched, it adheres rigorously to a fundamental structure of Mallarmé's poetry. That structure is characterized by a scene split between a reality unbearable in its sheer boredom (and whose characteristic color is white), on the one hand, and a taboo dream intolerable in its intensity (and whose characteristic color is a waning red against a backdrop of azure), on the other. It will be seen that the only viable place for the poem, given the impossibility of either dream or reality, is the line or partition dividing one from the other. One approaches the forbidden dream paradoxically, by taking one's metaphorical distance from it.

Consider now, as a further instantiation of the structure just adduced, "L'Après-midi d'un faune." In the mythical beast's attempted reconstruction of the key episode in the poem, the faun pursues the "animal whiteness" of two sister nymphs locked in erotic embrace, dives—at high noon—into the glaucous Sicilian pond to begin the chase. At which point, the nymph-like whiteness gives way to red-hot excitement (*"tout brûle dans l'heure fauve"*). The contemporary reader may be thinking Debussy (as opposed to Wagner), but he is simultaneously drawn to the almost abstract color scheme split by the discontinuity between the whiteness of the *moire* covers draping the overstuffed furniture of the traditional theater and the "swooning gold" of the trumpets—i.e., a scheme identical to that of the poem of homage to Wagner himself.

And then, as if to confirm our reading, at noon itself, the faun commits the error of disentangling (or dividing) the two sisterly nymphs, one timid in the "candor" of her "feathery whiteness," but soon to be tickled by the faun into red-hot excitement. Whereupon the two nymphs escape the rape attempt, leaving the faun to his erotic fiasco. Everything hinges on the split between a dead whiteness and an all too ambitious (or intense) crimson, figuring the taboo dream.

But it is at this juncture that I would note that my persistent interest in *Adventures in the French Trade* lay in a potential epitaph, said to be one to die for, in the form of a very brief quatrain by Mallarmé honoring the poet's friend Louis Metman, founding director of the Musée des arts décoratifs. It is in fact dedicated to the poet's verse itself:

> Tant de luxe où l'or se moire
> N'égale pas, croyez-m'en,
> Vers! dormir en la mémoire
> De Monsieur Louis Metman,

All that shimmering gold, we read, would not be equal to the luxury of reposing in the recesses of the memory of the poet's friend. (And the friend's name was such, I reported, as to be replaceable by my own without violating the prosody of the poem. Whence the link between slumber, *dormir*, dreams, and the post-humously perceived coherence of Mallarmé's poetry…) All this was offered in my initial memoir as grounds for enlisting Mallarmé's apparently trivial quatrain as an imaginary epitaph for the author (Metman/Mehlman). But on second reading I am inclined to observe that the rhyme *moire /mémoire* also happens to appear in Mallarmé's poem of "Hommage" to Wagner. And that the reference to furniture (*mobilier*) in the Wagner poem seems to link up with the focus of Metman's celebrated Musée des arts décoratifs. To which we would add that the poem appears to be an epitaph (or Tombeau) for Wagner himself…

Of the Mallarméan poems toying with poetry's relation to music, the one that intersects most tellingly with "L'après-midi d'un faune" is titled "Sainte." It evokes two images of Saint Cecilia, patron saint of music and "musicienne du silence." One has her playing a viola (*viole*), the other play-ing a harp, as each instrument takes shape consecutively in the shifting light refracted through the stained glass image of a monstrance. The poem, that is, enacts the separation of the two sister images of Saint Cecilia even as it would cohere with the Faun's separation of the two nymphs at high noon in an experience of erotic failure. The case is clinched in two instances: first, the failed rape (*viol*) in its Sicilian setting is a transformation of the viola (*viole*) initially played by the stained-glass Saint Cecilia; secondly, the Faun's finger in Sicily titillates the "feathery white" nymph until she blushes red even as the digit of the Saint's finger is poised over the instrumental plumage of the harp (which may in fact be, in its shape, the wing of a passing angel).

Thus the (failed) rape is identical in structure to the monstrance in the church. Or rather it takes place (or fails to) within the Catholic relic of a monstrance. The quintessential Mallarméan configuration of *"L'après-midi d'un faune"* with or as "Sainte" is tantamount to a fouling of the monstrance, a desecration of the wafer that is Christ's body incarnate. The question remains, however, one of the interpretation of that intricate overlap of, say, the hypothetical *viol* in Sicily and the potential *viole* being played by Saint Cecilia. Is it a desecration of the wafer of Christ's body implemented by the (Jewish) critic's own ingenuity and thus a warrant for anti-semitic sentiment itself? (Or is it, to the extent that the interpretation of Mallarmé is altogether convincing, an attack on Christianity staged by a poet convinced that Poetry was the new religion or liturgy destined to subvert it?) The pages that follow will be inclined to focus on that first interpretation: the ingenuity of the Jewish critic productive of a fantasy—of a fouling of the monstrance—said to fuel antisemitism itself.

These considerations, we have observed, were related to music as it figures, but in a way never made quite explicit, in *Adventures in the French Trade*: it involves a deep connection between music and the suffering of the Jew. Nowhere is that connection made more explicit than in Anthony Julius's gloss on a line out of *Lamentations*: "I am their musick," meaning that music, in at least one of its Biblical roots, is a protracted celebration of the mockery and suffering of the Jew as recorded and reacted to in *Lamentations*.[5]

**

The threat—specifically to Jews—posed by music as performed by a devastatingly talented brother; its apparent manifestation in a French poet's fantasy of Wagner; the almost masochistic pleasure derived from the author's

---

5 Anthony Julius, *Trials of the Diaspora: A History of Anti-Semitism in England* (Oxford: Oxford University Press, 2010), p. 149.

critical construction of just such a threat; the historical embodiment of that construction, in the broad sense, in a reading of the German occupation of France in World War II and, more narrowly, in the career of a superstar of occupied Paris become a leading conductor of post-war Boston… All these elements tend to converge in Quignard's eponymous essay in the volume he called *"La haine de la musique."* It insists on Primo Levi's observation about Auschwitz: "In the *Lager* music drew us downward."[6] It elaborates music's relation to the unshielded—lidless—character of music's ear in a meditation on a link between "aesthetic pleasure and sadistic *jouissance*" that has everything in common with the "masochistic pleasure" of the author's blissful construction—as criticism— of a historical threat against the Jews. In Quignard's formulation: "Music hurts [La musique fait mal.]"[7]

**

One measure of the oddity of the critic's masochistic relation to literature was said critic's appearance as a character in Malcolm Bradbury's novel *My Strange Quest for Mensonge.* The episode is briefly evoked in *Adventures in the French Trade*, about a deconstructionist so radical as to self-deconstruct, with the result that the protagonist spends much of a novel attempting unsuccessfully to track him down. All to no avail: every examination of the indexes of a generation's guides to criticism yields the name Merleau-Ponty preceded by Mehlman, with Mensonge, no where to be found, in between. As though Mensonge himself were no more than the discontinuous blank separating the two proper names. And it is a blank whose nebulousness is not beyond contaminating those that surround it: the novel's imaginary index contains a line that reads: "Mehlman, Jeffrey, his role in indexes."

Now just as an operation on my eyelids seemed strategically to follow, in a second volume, the green-light laser focused on my prostate in the first, so Laurent Binet's *La Septième fonction du langage*, the novel into which I was incorporated, as evoked in this second volume, follows my inclusion in *Adventures in the French Trade*, as an importation from Malcolm Bradbury's *Strange*

---

6 Quignard, p. 201.
7 Ibid, p. 218.

Quest for Mensonge.[8] Moreover, as we shall see, just as my name, like "Mensonge" in Bradbury's book, seemed to be caught up in a difference between what was alphabetically too early ("Mehlman") and alphabetically too late ("Merleau-Ponty"), just so my name seemed to be split in two.

Binet's novel, winner of the Prix Interallié, is centered on the speculative possibility that Roland Barthes, who died as a result of being run over by a laundry van, had in fact been assassinated by whoever had stolen the text that Barthes had happened to have been reading as he crossed the street at the time of his apparent accident. That text is said in the novel to be an unpublished fragment by Roman Jakobson discussing a variety of speech act capable of imposing itself on whomever it addresses and thus of considerable political import.

Now Binet invents as the climactic sequence of his novel a colloquium said to be held at Cornell University (and in fact modeled on the colloquium at Johns Hopkins said to mark the conquest of American intellectual life by French structuralist "theory"). The chapter (58) of the novel begins with the alleged program of the all-star colloquium, with its nineteen French and American speakers, held at Ithaca and featuring the likes of Derrida (on "A sec solo") and Foucault (on "Jeux de polysémie dans l'onirocritique d' Artémidore"), but also the likes of Chomsky, Searle, and myself. My own subject was titled "Blanchot, the laundry man." (Significantly—a sign of the times?—Americans in this French novel, published in 2016, when they speak, do so in English. The novel itself, that is, might well have served as the subject of a chapter in—the allegedly anti-American—Régis Debray's recent volume, *Civilisation: Comment nous sommes devenus américains*.)[9] The fictive title of my talk at the imaginary conference in Ithaca would have been recognized by my readers in terms of the suspicions of a white-washing (*blanchisserie*) of the political past of Maurice Blanchot, whose writings, during the 1930s, including a call to acts of terrorism against Jews and Communists, had long since been banned from mention in the world of French letters, where Blanchot was the object of a cult. Some of the complications of my own challenge to that ban were invoked in the central chapter ("Chiasmus") of the first volume of my *Adventures in the French Trade*. To which we will return…

---

8 Laurent Binet, *La septième fonction du langage* (Paris: Librairie générale française, 2016).
9 Régis Debray, *Comment sommes-nous devenus américains* (Paris: Gallimard, 2017).

But the fictive title "Blanchot, the laundry man" served as an (undeveloped?) potential link to the central plot of *La septième fonction du langage*. For that book, as already mentioned, was centered on the death of Roland Barthes as a result of his being run over by a laundry van while reading an unpublished text by Roman Jakobson (on a politically invaluable "seventh function of language").

In addition to "Jeffrey Mehlman," as "he" (or "I") is called in Binet's novel, "I" appears as well as a young man in Ithaca called simply "Jeffrey." He or I appears most strikingly in an exchange with the philosopher John Searle, also said to be present at the Ithaca colloquium. As "I" passes by a table at which Searle is seated, he hails me (like a cab): "Hey, Jeffrey, you must translate for me the last piece of trash of the asshole." "I" responds: "Hey, John, I'm not your bitch. You do it yourself, OK?" Now the reason I know that the "Jeffrey" so addressed is "me" himself is that the exchange reads as a truculent transposition—half Tarantino, half *Fight Club*—of an episode that actually is recorded in my first volume of *Adventures in the French Trade*. Briefly stated: During a year (1974-1975) as a visiting faculty member at Berkeley, at a time I believed it my mission to convert whoever on the West coast was prepared to listen to me as purveyor of the good news (the thought of Derrida) streaming out of Paris by way of Baltimore and New Haven, I was surprised to realize that the person most interested in what I had to say was the philosopher John Searle. At the time, I had failed to realize that Searle's posture was that of a philosophical cop, eager to gather information about the alleged malfeasance of Derrida of a sort that could be used to prosecute him for some variant of philosophical fraud. As soon as I realized what was at stake, I withdrew from the reading group several of us had formed in the hills of Berkeley. And that withdrawal finds its precise equivalent, outrageously transposed, in the line "I'm not your bitch, John." In brief, the chapter on my role in Derrida's polemic with Searle, an oft cited episode in the history of criticism, became the source of a memorable scene in Binet's novel, which in turn became a scene in this second series of adventures in the French trade…

**

The surgical procedure affecting my eyesight, and its unexpected dovetailing with a prior surgery at the beginning of my adventures in the French trade, brings to mind an entire book of mine whose very title was generated from a case of experimental surgery on a subject whose vision was gravely defective. The book, my third, was called *Cataract: An Essay in Diderot.*[10] It was born of an eighteenth century experiment on the removal of the cataracts of a patient born blind. And the epistemological question raised by such an experiment was whether its subject would be able to match a sphere or cube known only by touch with corresponding figures known only through visual perception.

The figure of the "cataract" was tripartite: the first component being an image of chaos or cloud, such as the one blocking (clarity of) vision; the second, the permanence of a barrier (or dike) which, in its self-sameness, impedes its spill into randomness; and the third, which is an expenditure of the very *being* of whatever might be contained by the dike as cataract: the downward current or spiral of the informational equivalent of entropy. Articulate the three versions of the cataract and one finds oneself immersed in a structure or system (or, better yet, *syrrhem*) that is fundamentally meteorological . Such is the formula of Michel Serres in an essay on Barbey d'Aurevilly: "there are clouds [*des nuages*], then rain, and then comes everything [*et voilà tout*]."[11] That meteorology figures a general case of which astronomy offers a limited (and reversible) instance. It is also a gloss on the thought of Lucretius, about whom Michel Serres wrote a particularly inventive book. And finally it weaves Diderot into a genealogy that draws Lucretius toward a strange fulfillment in Serres.

Now one of the oddest features of the affinity established between Diderot and Lucretius is that in my reading of Diderot, "Analyse spectrale," the Serres text on which it draws most compellingly, is a reading not of Lucretius but of the nineteenth century reactionary and proto-decadent Barbey d'Aurevilly. The fit—between reactionary Barbey and liberal Diderot—seems formally perfect, but ideologically incoherent. And the tolerance of that incoherence is a defect of perception, or so it seemed to me, every bit as glaring as the one haunting the experiment on blindness that figures at the inception of my *Cataract.*

---

10 Jeffrey Mehlman, *Cataract: An Essay in Diderot* (Middletown, CT: Wesleyan University Press, 1979).

11 Michel Serres, "Analyse spectrale" in *Hermès IV, La Distribution* (Paris: Minuit, 1977), pp. 213-255.

Years later I learned of the existence of a work by Barbey d'Aurevilly titled *Goethe et Diderot,* but hesitated to read it. For I found it hard to imagine that any encounter between Barbey and Diderot (or rather the impasse of any such encounter) could not but function as a refutation of whatever I had constructed in *Cataract.*

And then I read the Barbey text and the unexpected escape from what I took to be an ineluctable impasse dawned on me. The solution of my dilemma came with a triangulation of the binary opposition between Diderot and Voltaire. For whereas Voltaire, in his investment in astronomy, embodied an idealized reversibility, everything about Diderot, "opposed in every way to Voltaire," as perceived by Barbey, seemed to dispense a Germanic or thermodynamic decline into the cool chaos of Goethe…[12] Diderot, "was the turbulent streaming of speech, falling ceaselessly from the high point of a steaming head."[13] He resembles "fountains ceaselessly releasing their violent flow."[14] And the destination of that cataract is the "the chill of Goethe, who perishes in all his works because of the cold." Diderot, according to Barbey, marks, via Goethe, the Germanization of French thought.[15] And the entire process is simultaneously, at every cycle of the spiral, a figure of decadence itself. The apparent imperfection, in sum, of my reading of Diderot *via* Barbey is simultaneously a completion, supplement, or, better yet, delineation of the contours of Serres's reading of Lucretius.

**

There would, over the years, be other supplements and/as complements, perhaps even endgames, enacting—or reversing *in extremis*—phases of my work. One would entail the long polemic in which I have been involved in the course of my essays on the political writings of Maurice Blanchot. It may be recalled that one of the turning points of that engagement involved a letter to the *Quinzaine littéraire* by Mathieu Bénézet claiming that only an American would stoop to the depths to which I had allegedly sunk in my essay on Blanchot at *Combat.*

---

12 Barbey d'Aurevilly, *Goethe et Diderot* (Paris: Ligaran, 2016), p. 126.
13 Ibid, p. 115.
14 Ibid., p. 165.
15 Ibid., p. 126.

Bénézet claimed that the Célinophiles of *Tel quel* had been so compromised by their cult of Céline that they hired out an American goon (presumably myself) to rough Blanchot up. The configuration was very much that of Milan Kundera's luminous novel of the same period, *The Unbearable Lightness of Being*: "too cowardly to write such an article [on collaboration, objective guilt, and the myth of Oedipus themselves), they had hidden behind a naïve doctor."[16] Such would be the Communist case for convincing Kundera's protagonist to retract his critique of those Czechs who pleaded innocence or ignorance in their collaboration with a Soviet puppet regime. Bénézet, moreover, the author of the polemical piece in the *Quinzaine littéraire*, had long been affiliated with the French Communist Party.

Another characteristic of the Oedipus episode in Kundera's novel is the fact that the publishers of the protagonist's article had mangled his text: "without asking him, [the editors] shortened his text by so much that it was reduced to its basic thesis (making it too schematic and aggressive). He didn't like it anymore."[17] Curiously, the Kunderian refusal to challenge the mangling of his text, no doubt out of loyalty to its emblematic status as an (almost Camusian) instance of the absurdity of life in Communist Prague, found its counterpart in my own refusal to challenge the absurdity of a line misattributed to me in an article in *Newsweek* and related to the Blanchot episode. My text in *Tel quel*, it may be recalled, had been quite poorly translated, "mangled," as it were, but I immediately challenged the numerous misrenderings in a letter to the editor (Philippe Sollers) of the journal. And the list of errata with which my letter concluded ended up as the final pages of *Tel quel*, which was just then changing its name (to *L'Infini*) and its publisher (from Seuil to Denoël).

But a second article, appearing in *Newsweek* shortly thereafter, seems to follow the Kunderian prototype more loyally.[18] Shortly after what has been called the Blanchot "affair," a second "affair," centered on the wartime journalism of Paul de Man, included an interview with me, which was prompted by a widespread assumption that the de Man affair was a remake of the Blanchot affair. Having previously commented at length on the argument of Jean Paulhan

---

16 Milan Kundera, *The Unbearable Lightness of Being* (New York: Harper & Row, 1984), translated by M. H. Heim, p. 191.
17 Ibid., p. 178.
18 Newsweek, February 15, 1988.

that given the fact that French *résistants* had spent a good part of the pre-war period rehearsing an imagined collaboration with Russia's communists, and French collaborationists had spent a good part of the pre-war period rehearsing their resistance to Communists, there could be no moral high ground between the two options. Indeed, that the whole of deconstruction, rooted as it was in just such a chiasmus or criss-cross, could be read as a vast amnesty project for acts of resistance and collaboration during the war. But it was here that a decisive mangling of my argument was introduced; for it was suggested that what was at stake was a vast amnesty project "for acts of collaboration" during the war. The chiasmus was elided and transformed into a whitewash. And I was in short order cast in the role of an enemy of deconstruction. I felt myself to be above all deluded in my belief that I might summarize convincingly my chiastic argument in a brief interview and thus, even more so, in a letter to the editor of a popular weekly, and so refrained from responding, lest I find myself in a situation as emblematically absurd as that befalling the text on Oedipus (and objective guilt) in its mangled form in Kundera's novel.

There was in sum a tripartite construct in Kundera's masterpiece that meshed rigorously with my own misimplication in the Blanchot "affair." The first consisted of the numerous misrenderings of the translation of my essay "Blanchot at *Combat*: Literature and Terror" in *Tel Quel* as they might be articulated with an editor's errors in the publication of the protagonist's essay on Oedipus, collaboration, and objective guilt. The second was related to Bénézet's accusation in *la Quinzaine littéraire* that I had been commissioned by *Tel quel*'s adepts of an antisemitic Céline to lambaste Blanchot as it might be articulated with the efforts of party bureaucrats to get Kundera's protagonist to retract that same essay. And the third related to my failure to contest the truncated version of my reading of the chiasmus linking "collaboration" and "resistance" in David Lehman's article on the deMan affair in *Newsweek* as it might be articulated with the failure of Kundera's protagonist to contest the severe truncation of his argument.

Add to the mix that a Kundera surrogate in *The Unbearable Lightness* was victim of editorial impingement and that Kundera himself was being published in the 1980s in *L'Infini* by Philippe Sollers, that is: in the very journal (and by the very editor) that played a key role in the publication of the defective translation of my essay "Blanchot at *Combat*," and the nexus (or network) appears complete.

**

My speculations on the thrust of Blanchot's political writings of the 1930s were bound to encounter the work of Derrida and specifically Derrida's commentary on Blanchot's narrative of the end of the war, *L'Instant de ma mort*, which he called *Demeure*. My unpublished response to *Demeure* took the form of a letter to Pierre Assouline, whose "République des livres," his blog for *Le Monde* at the time, featured a spirited endorsement of my engagement with Blanchot's political writings of the 1930s. From my letter to Assouline:

> Strange book: I had become used to being told that it was naïve, deconstructively speaking, to tie so much to a date— October 1938, Munich, *'L'Arrêt de mort,'* Iphigenia, the farewell to fascism, etc; and here we find JD wanting to tie even more to a date, July 20, 1944: (p. 119, "All formulations taking the form of "X without X" find their possibility… in what transpired on that day, at that precise instant.)
>
> In opposing what he calls Blanchot's "political prosecutors" (including myself, I suppose; cf. p. 57), he naïvely turns into a lawyer for the defense. This gives formulations such as: "The author might count himself as a member of the Resistance… He waged war against…genocidal antisemites" (p. 92) To which I would say: better, politically speaking, to be seen as breaking in 1938 with a fascism that is acknowledged (the theme of my essay 'Iphigenia 38') than to be flaunting the fact that one may have been confusedly thought of as being associated with the Resistance in July 1944, which is very late indeed.
>
> Here's another take on 'Demeure': The book contains a long development on "seven trajectories" of the word "passion" in MB's work. But what about an eighth case: the 1936 text "La grande passion des modérés" in COMBAT? It meshes perfectly with all JD's developments about "pas" and is inspired by Bernanos' (best-selling) polemic, *La grande peur des bien-pensants*. Whereby I would fold JD's analysis of MB, admirable in its own terms, into my own…

There is more, of course: the centrality of the reference to Paulhan—Paulhan "whose face, fate, role, thought and writing bring together, during and after the war, a significant share of the political tangle we are presently discussing" (133)—in JD's reading of l'"Instant de ma mort" meshes with the role he is made to play in my "Writing and Deference." Just as the equivalence of what the Nazis did to MB in 1944 and what the French did to Hegel in 1806 ("a turn and return of circumstances at once just and unjust" p. 111) seems a motif worthy of Paulhan (if not of the Montherlant of 'Solstice de juin'!)...

The principal effort to neutralize my reading of Blanchot as sometime antisemite—beyond Derrida's attempt (as encapsulated in my e-mail to Assouline just summarized)—took the form of a would-be *Festschrift* that failed to materialize due to the withdrawal of a number of contributors once they had encountered my essay in *Tel quel*. The principal casualties of the abandoned *Festschrift*, an issue of *Cahiers de l'Herne* intended to be dedicated to Blanchot in the 1980s, were the editorial team composed of Philippe Lacoue-Labarthe and Jean-Luc Nancy, each of them humiliated by the apparent fiasco, and who were joined by Mathieu Bénézet (a name we have already encountered in the polemic against me in *La Quinzaine littéraire*). Lacoue-Labarthe's volume, *Agonie terminée et agonie interminable: Sur Maurice Blanchot* (2011), more or less begins with a letter to Blanchot proposing the volume to honor him as a corrective to the attention accorded to my essay (however poorly translated!) in *Tel quel*.[19] But by the end of his volume, the reader is treated to the text of a lecture delivered by Lacoue-Labarthe in Japan in the course of which he all but abjures Derrida's position and rallies to the position I had maintained in my various essays on the early political writing of Blanchot (with 1938 and 1942-43 as turning points). As for Nancy, his book *Maurice Blanchot: Passion politique* (2011) more or less begins— *"bien sûr,"* as he puts it—with a reference to my *Legacies: Of Antisemitism in France*.[20] Yet before long, we find, in Nancy's text, an acknowledgment of the components of an anti-semitic discourse in Blanchot: "What remains is the antisemitism, or what one would have a hard

---

19 *Agonie terminée et agonie interminable: Sur Maurice Blanchot* (Paris: Galilée, 2011), p. 16.
20 *Maurice Blanchot: Passion politique* (Paris: Galilée, 2011). p. 10.

time designating as anything else even if it might coincide with realities that are quite different. It was rare and restricted in Blanchot, But it was ..."[21] The humiliating collapse of a discourse opposed to my own on the political writings of the first Blanchot is thus to be found in the works of France's two leading acolytes of Derrida even as the elements of a deconstruction of *L'Instant de ma mort* were to be found in the e-mail I sent to Assouline and that I have included above.

And then, in 2015, a protracted essay in literary history titled *L'autre Blanchot: l'écriture de jour, l'écriture de nuit* was published by Michel Surya at Gallimard. It summarizes the history of Blanchot's efforts to chronicle his relation to his own political past in terms of two elusive letters. The first was a letter to me responding to a question voiced in my letter of 1979 to Blanchot on his past and which read: "Am I completely off the track" [[Me suis-je complètement fourvoyé]?" (Blanchot 's answer focused on a single incident in order to be able to reply in the affirmative.) The second letter was addressed by Blanchot in 1984 to Roger Laporte, would provide the bulk of the text of Nancy's *Maurice Blanchot: passion politique*, and was taken by Surya to be irreducibly mendacious, insisting as it does on Blanchot's alleged rejection (or refusal) of Pétain and Vichy from the outset of the new regime, a rejection belied by a virulently pro-Vichy editorial appearing in Aux écoutes under the name of the director of that right-wing publication, Maurice Blanchot.[22]

Surya subsequently makes reference to an unpublished letter addressed "encore et toujours indirectement à Mehlman."[23] It is a curious notation since the actual addressee of the letter is not even identified—as though what interested Surya was more the obliqueness or indirection—or unconsciousness—of my relation to its text than its explicit properties. Still further on in Surya's chronicle, particular attention is paid to Blanchot's commentary—"Les intellectuels en question"—on Jean-Denis Bredin's history of the Dreyfus Affair, a book that I happen to have translated into English.[24] A constellation joining antisemitism, the Nazi genocide, and French nationalism informs Blanchot's discussion of the Affair. Blanchot is said to "appear to endorse the central and— no matter what has been said on the subject—irrefutable [*imparable*] argument

---

21 Ibid., pp. 33-34.
22 *Aux écoutes*, July 1942.
23 Surya, p. 54.
24 Maurice Blanchot, "Les Intellectuels en question" in *Le Débat*, 20, March 1984.

of Mehlman (to whom 'Les intellectuels en question' constitutes in part a coded reply), and according to which the excesses of German Nazi criminality had the effect of dispelling the 'measure' of the French fascist crime…""[25] Once again the relation to events entertained by my text is one of "encryption," "indirection," or unconsciousness. And Surya may indeed have been right. When I first read Blanchot's essay, I could not help thinking that his inability to fathom the compatibility between the viciousness of the Affair and the literary finesse of, say, the antidreyfusard Paul Valéry, seemed almost to be a version of my own difficulty in fathoming the compatibility between early and late Blanchot.

Might there not be, I found myself thinking, a significance attached to the fact that the final chapter of Surya's book consists of a passage cited from Blanchot's "Les intellectuels en question," the very essay interpreted by Surya as an encrypted reply to the central argument in my essays on the political evolution of Blanchot. It reads as follows: "There might thus be in every life a moment in which what is least justifiable carries the day and what is incomprehensible receives its due."[26]

If my "endgame" with Blanchot, as one may be tempted to call it, is terminal in a significant sense, it is by way of the fate of what might be called Bénézet's implicit call, at the beginning of play, for a retraction in the *Quinzaine littéraire* of the position I was espousing in *Tel quel* (and in English in *Modern Language Notes*[27]). For Surya's book on Blanchot, a work written in "encrypted" counterpoint with my own essays on Blanchot, was reviewed in *la Quinzaine littéraire* by Frédéric Postel in an essay that ended with a statement of support for my position. In Postel's concluding remark: "As it stands, *L'Autre Blanchot* suffices. To do what? To perturb its readers by inviting them to reflect on the inconsistency (*inconséquence*) of human thought The reception of this book will thus not be without its moments of rejection. Let us hope that they will be less violent than those that confronted Jacques Lecarme in 2003 and, before him, Jeffrey Mehlman at the time of the publication of *Legacies: Of Anti-Semitism* in France (1983)."[28]

---

25 Surya, p. 97.

26 Ibid., p. 124

27 "Blanchot at Combat: Of Literature and Terror" in *MLN* 95 (4), May 1980.

28 Frédéric Postel, "Maurice Blanchot, sans guillemets" in *La Quinzaine Littéraire* (Paris, May 15, 2015).

The *Quinzaine littéraire* of 2015, in sum, had reversed—through Fré-déric Postel—the judgment on my reading of Blanchot first formulated in *La Quinzaine littéraire* by Mathieu Bénézet (in 1982). It is a reversal consolidated in Surya's book on the "other Blanchot," moreover—a development connected to the poem of Leconte de Lisle titled "Sûryâ" and set to music as a symphonic can-tata by one Alfred Bachelet, head of the musical group named "Collaboration" during World War II. And as if to consolidate that very consolidation, we are left with the pun, *Surya*, the author of the book exonerating me on the subject of the evolution of Blanchot's political thought, as *Sûryâ*, France's would-be wartime response to Wagner, the symphonic cantata received in 1942, under the baton of Charles Munch, France's soon-to-be gift to musical Boston, as the masterpiece of the honorary president of the musical section of the Groupe Collaboration.

All this brings us—via my own skewed relation to the case of Blan-chot—to an apparently random configuration haunting this chapter, and perhaps this volume: the connection between French anti-semitism and the world of classical music. But at this point it is difficult for me not to recall an impression visited on me at the time the Blanchot "affair" erupted in the early 1980s. It concerns my undertaking the translation of Bredin's classic his-tory of the Dreyfus Affair, *L'Affaire*.[29] It was a deeply moving effort, which had me at one point interrupting my work because I found myself weeping profusely. Years passed and I remembered that temporary cessation of my work on the Bredin volume, even as I had forgotten precisely which episode had had that effect on me. And then, years later, I found myself attending a lecture at Cardozo Law School delivered by Dreyfus' grandson, Charles. He stated that Dreyfus himself preferred not to speak about his ordeal during the approxi-mately quarter of a century that separated his pardon from his death, but that the one incident that he never quite put behind him was the discovery during his second trial (at Rennes) that the Army Chief of Staff, Boisdeffre, who had presented himself to Dreyfus as a sympathizer during his ordeal, was in fact a principal architect of the fraudulent case against him. It was upon hearing that confession of how undone the Captain apparently was by the betrayal of Bois-deffre at Rennes that I recalled that such was precisely the episode in Bredin's history that had me setting aside my effort, unable as I was to continue.

---

29 Jean-Denis Bredin, *The Affair: The Case of Alfred Dreyfus* (New York: Braziller, 1986), trans-lated by J. Mehlman.

Now the other idiosyncratic memory of the experience of translating *L'Affaire* was mediological in nature. It concerned the fact that I was working for the first time on a word processor. It was a primitive and unwieldy unit, bearing the brand name Kaypro, and I came to realize, as I made my way through the 628 pages of the book, that my exercise of transcribing page by page, French to English, was an approximation of my pianist brother's talent as a sight-reader. I at the Kaypro, in theory, would outclass my brother at his Steinway, a feat all the more striking in what Pontalis might have called its *férocité* in that the Dreyfus Affair, given the exemplary participation of Mathieu Dreyfus, Alfred's loyal brother, was itself a drama of fraternal devotion.[30]

All this allows us to assemble an intersection of various conceptual and affective strands that we have in fact isolated earlier in these pages in our charting of a nodal point in *Adventures in the French Trade:* French anti-semitism (via the Dreyfus Affair); a conflictual relation between music and print (via a gifted pianist's ability to sight-read and a budding translator's emerging skill with a word processor); and the flickering *férocité* affecting a saga of brotherly love. That all these elements should coverge *en route* to the conclusion of Surya's volume on Blanchot's vexed relation to a particularly cruel component of his own political past—but "Surya" was the title of a symphonic cantata composed toward the outset of World War II by the honorary president of the musical section of the Groupe Collaboration—entailed a displacement of his discussion of Blanchot from the context of occupied France to that of the Dreyfus Affair toward the end of his career in "Les intellectuels en question," a text that Surya interprets as an "encrypted response" (but also a " concession") to the "unanswerable" *—imparable*—"central argument" of my essays on Blanchot. The entire configuration brings me as close to an intuition of the "unconscious" of *Adventures in the French Trade* as I am likely to get.

**

A discussion of my relation to the question of Blanchot's political history figured as the first of four analytic sequences in what I termed the central chapter, titled "Chiasmus," of *Adventures in the French Trade*. The sequences

---

30 J-B- Pontalis, *Frère du précédent* (Paris: Gallimard, 2006).

were elaborated from most recent to most originary and took the form, drawing on a conceit of Paul Morand, of postmarks to be construed on the anonymous letter my life might have been. In that earlier book, the first sequence presented, postmarked "Boston 1983," focused on Blanchot and situated his political evolution—from anti-semitic to philo-semitic—within the twisting topology of a Möbius strip generated by a superimposition of the mental universes of Edouard Drumont, author of *La France juive* and patron saint of French anti-semitism; Georges Bernanos, self-proclaimed disciple of Drumont and author of *La grande peur des bien-pensants*, a volume that celebrated Drumont even as Bernanos effected a subsequent transition (in *Les grands cimetières sous la lune*) to anti-fascism; and Maurice Clavel, whose mental universe was deeply dependent on the writing of Bernanos even as he, Clavel, pursued a vision that was fundamentally philo-semitic. The preceding pages of this essay are a kind of post-script to the "Boston 1983" section of "Chiasmus" and constitute a kind of endgame played out in the wake of the position I had staked out in the course of what has been called the Blanchot affair.

After Blanchot and the chiasmus—or Möbius strip—within which I found myself functioning, the second such configuration I found myself negotiating bore the label (or coordinates) : "Paris 1970." Its subject was Jean Laplanche's stellar reading of Freud, an interpretation whose horizon, Laplanche once wrote me, much to my shock, was to "demolish" Freud. Laplanche's analysis of Freud was pursued through a series of doubly inscribed terms, each a piece in one of two battling interpretative schemes. Now of those schemes, one persisted in ignorance or innocence of the other and came to flourish or (as Lacan might have put it) fester as an "ego psychology" of a decidedly American ilk. The other, which would thrive as a variant of what might be called French structuralism, mediated nothing so much as a theory of the inevitability of the error entailed by the opposing interpretative scheme.

Now the emblem of that scheme is the configuration of a chiasmus or criss-cross pressed into service at the end of *Vie et mort en psychanalyse*, which I translated and prefaced in 1976. Everything is mediated by a shift that takes the "pleasure principle," the soul of libidinal circulation in the unconscious, into its new role of naming the nourishing principle of Eros, as it builds larger and larger libidinal units, i.e., as it ultimately comes to figure the narcissistically constituted ego, a reality on the side of repression rather than on that of what is repressed. The unconscious, in sum, is construed as a structure in Laplanche's argument, a chiasmus enabling but also vitiating every speech act, deemed to be the province of the ego.

And then, in a volume titled *Nouveaux fondements pour la psychanalyse* and published by Laplanche in 1987, a reversal occurred.[31] The "new foundation" for psychoanalysis was to be "seduction," construed as a sexually freighted parental speech act, implanted in the child, poorly understood, and which the child may spend the rest of his life translating, de-translating, and retranslating… The unconscious is no longer the interface of a drive peeled off the interiority of the instinct, as it meshes with the speech act of seduction (proffered by an other), but that speech act as it *supplants* the drive "propped" on its instinct. The stabilizing function of structure (or myth) partakes of the ego and the narcissism that fuels it even as the unconscious, rooted in what Baudelaire might have called the *confuses paroles* of the other, abandons the column of structure for that of the speech act.

Laplanche's endgame, then, became a reversal of what was, in fact, originally the reverse return of a structuring chiasmus. This volume will contain an enigmatic assessment by Laplanche, shortly before his death, of what he one day called my *amours antisémites*. It will function as a nodal intersection of my own unconscious and Laplanche's and, as such, as close as the author of these pages has come to being analyzed from within the French analytic dispensation he has spent years expounding.

The third interpretative episode in "Chiasmus," the central chapter of *Adventures in the French Trade*, is labeled "Aix-en-Provence, 1966" and is devoted to my debt to the teacher who has most deeply influenced me, Charles Mauron, during the year I spent as a Fulbright scholar in Aix-en-Provence. It was distinguished by my growing enthrallment with Mauron's technique, inspired by Francis Galton's use of an art of superimposition as a way of supplying the equivalent of those free associations which could not, of course, be delivered by authors after their death. What struck me most keenly was the volume devoted to the "work and life" of Racine, specifically the system of modulations of Racine's tragedies as they succeed each other almost musically.

---

31 Presses universitaires de France

Now if Racine was (after Mallarmé, an author we have encountered earlier and crucially in these pages) the occasion of the first full scale analysis via superimposition performed by Mauron, it was toward the end of his life that he published what was in some ways a *reprise* of that same effort, but one devoted to Giraudoux, one of the masters of twentieth century French theater (and the author who gave pride of place to his essay on Racine in his programmatic volume titled *Littérature*). That circumstance resulted in an exercise on my part (in *Legacies: Of Anti-Semitism in France*) inspired by the superimposability of what might be called Racine's endgame and Giraudoux's. For just as Racine's *Athalie*—a Biblically inspired play, centered on the passions and delusions of the Biblical queen whom Giraudoux called *la vieillarde*—came as something of an endgame for the supreme playwright of the seventeenth century, so *La Folle de Chaillot*, the play about a mad female leader of the zanies of her neighborhood in Paris, came—posthumously—at the end of Giraudoux's career and figured as *his* endgame.

Athalie relates a successful plot on the part of the Jews to lure the demented queen of the northern kingdom—who, for dynastic reasons, entertains plans to do away with them—into a trap that will do away with *her* at play's end. And Aurélie, Giraudoux's mad queen of Chaillot, however, is in charge of thwarting the plans of a venal syndicate, headed by someone known as *Le Président*, who is intent on taking control of the oil deposits thought to lie beneath the streets of one of the more charming neighborhoods of Paris. The Resistance to that plan consists of the neighborhood zanies led by the madwoman of Chaillot and her lieutenant, known as the Ragpicker. The Ragpicker, played by Louis Jouvet in the first performances of the play, has a singular obsession: Paris, he believes, is being invaded by an exploitative syndicate peopled by members of an alien race, an obsession fleshed out by Giraudoux in his pre-war warning, *Pleins pouvoirs*. In that book the foreign race was identified as the Jews. There is no mention of Jews per se in *La Folle de Chaillot*. On the other hand, the President of the syndicate intent on taking over Paris has two principal antecedents in Giraudoux's oeuvre: one is the "President" of the short play, *Cantique des Cantiques*, which means that the President is at some level the Solomon of a modernized *Song of Songs* and the syndicate—of *La Folle de Chaillot*—a population of Jews; the other is a character named Moïse (i.e., Moses) in Giraudoux's novel of 1927, *Eglantine*. (The links between President[s] and Moïse and the three works of Giraudoux in which they appear are established in the chapter of my *Legacies: Of Anti-Semitism in France* titled "A Future for *Andromaque:* Aryan and Jew in Giraudoux's France.")[32]

Thus while *Athalie* tells the tale of an entrapment and destruction of the demented queen who would implement a genocide of the Jews, Giraudoux's *La Folle de Chaillot*, considered in its full intertextuality, relates what I have called the revenge of Athalie. Giraudoux, during the years of the German occupation of France, gives his blessing to the entrapment and destruction of the alien race—of Jews—invading and occupying Paris.

It is here that I am tempted to revert to my role as memorialist. For *La Folle de Chaillot*, it turns out, plays an important role as a discreet intertext of American literature. I refer to *The Ghost Writer*, the first of Philip Roth's extraordinary Zuckerman novels.[33] One of the themes of that novel is the power of bogus accusations of Jewish self-loathing. Thus young Zuckerman finds himself tearfully challenged by his mother over his failure to withdraw from publication a short text titled "Higher Education," deemed by his father to broadcast stereotypical Jewish vices to the Gentile community. (Roth's novel is dedicated to Milan Kundera, whom we have already encountered, and the motif of withdrawal from publication is not unrelated to that of retraction in *The Unbearable Lightness of Being*, discussed above.) Zuckerman's mother, in tears, tries to convince her son of how "good" a Jewish boy he has always been, how far removed the streak of nastiness in the contested fiction is from the person he has always been. (The mother's *schmaltz*, her contesting of Zuckerman's purveying of *schmutz*, are homologous with the opposition of kitsch and shit in the Kundera novel just adduced). Whereupon she recalls a particular scene from Zuckerman's childhood: "When Grandma was dying, you wrote her a letter that was like a poem, it was like—like listening to French, it was so beautiful."[34] Some years later, an interview with Claudia Roth Pierpont established that the subject of the letter was the role Philip Roth had been assigned in a play, which turned out to be *La Folle de Chaillot*, and the role was the Ragpicker: "a very poor man, much like Grandpa

32 J. Mehlman, *Legacies of anti-Semitism in France* (Minneapolis: University of Minnesota, 1983), pp. 34-63.
33 *The Ghost Writer* (New York: Vintage, 1979).
34 *The Ghost Writer*, p. 107.

must have been when he first saw America. And like you and Grandpa, this poor man wants the world to be good."[35] What this means, of course, is that the role of the Ragpicker was simultaneously available to interpretation in terms of *schmaltz* (social idealism) and of *schmutz* (anti-semitism and its genocidal impulse). Both poles of the chiasmus, positive and negative, would be activated, even as would be the case in Laplanche's acknowledgment of the *amours antisémites* that he saw coursing through my first volume of "adventures in the French trade."

**

Finally, after the postmarks, in reverse order, of "Boston 1983," with its focus on shifts in the thinking of Blanchot; "Paris 1970," with its attentiveness to Laplanche's assignment to an exemplary role of the figure of chiasmus in understanding Freud's metapsychology; and "Aix-en-Provence 1966," with Mauron's rewriting of the fantasmatics of the plays of Racine and then of Giraudoux, we arrive at the originary configuration of the central chapter, "Chiasmus," of my first volume of *Adventures in the French Trade.* Its postmark (on the anonymous letter I might construe my life as a—reading—writer to have been) was "Cambridge, 1927." Its subject was Charles Mauron's status as Bloomsbury's favorite French intellectual—from Virginia Woolf's attestation that she felt that she was likely to learn more from Mauron about writing than from anyone in England to E. M. Forster's dedication of his Clark Lectures of 1927, which would end up as the classic volume, *Aspects of the Novel.* It was Forster's dedication to Mauron of a book most provocatively about the figure of the criss-cross or chiasmus—Forster's "hourglass"—that enabled the topological space within which Forster managed to convey a sense of the anonymous letter my life as a reading writer may have been. It was Henry James' novel of 1903, *The Ambassadors,* which afforded Forster a plot in the shape of an hourglass, but one so rigorously choreographed as to fall short of that proclivity to betrayal without which the plot would feel "maimed," its characters "castrated." *The Ambassadors,* Forster opined, was of a structure more appropriate to the theater of Racine than of the European novel.

---

35 Claudia Roth Pierpont, *Roth Unbound* (New York: Farrar Straus, 2013), p. 260.

The chiasmus itself pits a character of diminished vitality, one Lambert Strether, who has been commissioned by his wealthy invalid widow of a *fiancée*, Mrs. Newsome, to take off to Paris, and bring back to Massachusetts her errant son, Chad, who has taken up with an aging Parisian beauty and paragon of elegance, Madame de Vionnet. The problem is that even as Chad has come to think that it is his time to return to a leadership position in the family business of manufacturing an inglorious object, just so does Lambert Strether come to realize, upon exposure to the increased refinement of Chad, that he would do well to remain in Paris and fight for (rather than against) its claims to constitute a superior civilization. Such would be the chiasmus of James' novel and just so would it be transferred—via Forster's dedication—to Mauron's criss-crossed reading of Racine, followed, in my reading, by Laplanche's take on the chiasmus structuring Freud's metapsychology, and the Möbius strip twisting one strand of its Drumont/Bernanos/Clavel genealogy around its other…

Now for all of Forster's impatience with James' novel, it is worth noting that Forster's novels entailed importantly oblique reactivations of the plot of *The Ambassadors*. Take his first novel, *Where Angels Fear to Tread*. Mrs Herriton, a suburban British matriarch, sends Philip, her milksop of a son, to Italy with a commission to rescue the infant son that his deceased sister-in-law, Lilia, had borne to her Italian lover, Gino, in a small Italian town modeled on San Gimignano. As in the James novel, rescuing the child before he is spoiled by the vulgarities of the Continent is the order of the day. At a crucial turn in the Forster novel, Philip, who has come to know a friendship of unprecedented intensity with Gino, finds himself stalked, and even tortured by Gino, who has learned of Philip's plan, ending disastrously, to kidnap his young relative back to England. Gino, in his rage, twists Philip's fractured arm in its socket, and the experience is of a force and intimacy previously unknown to him… Oddly enough, Forster's final novel, *A Passage to India*, involves a trip to a peninsula every bit as southern as Italy—namely India. A widowed British matriarch, one Mrs. Moore, travels to the subcontinent accompanied by Adela, slated to be the wife of Mrs. Moore's son, a colonial officer. Their *fiançailles* peter out virtually before they begin. Meanwhile, in a manner uncharacteristic of the British *raj*, Mrs. Moore befriends Dr. Aziz, a Muslim, for whom that friendship takes on great significance. Dr. Aziz himself becomes friends with a British educator stationed in India, named Fielding. That friendship, which will end up taking on more importance than his relation with Mrs. Moore, is initiated in a curious circumstance. Aziz arrives early to a reception at Fielding's lodging. The Englishman, emerging from a shower, discovers that he is lacking a stay—or "stud"—for the back hole of his shirt collar. Aziz volunteers to give up his stud and even to insert it in the rear hole of his shirt despite explicitly voiced fears that the stud may be too large for the hole. And thus begins the unconsummated romance of Forster's final (and most celebrated) novel. What is most striking in the context just adduced is its resonance with what turns out to be the culminating episode of Forster's first novel: i.e., the twisting of Philip's injured arm in its socket.

The episode of the stud will persist in *A Passage to India*, where the blindness of colonialist contempt will take the form of Mrs. Moore's son treating Aziz's failure to wear his rear stud as a result not of generosity, but of Indian slovenliness. That misinterpretation of the episode in the novel, its reading in terms of anticolonialism rather than sexual repression, is arguably of a piece with the history of the interpretation of what has been called one of the great novels of the twentieth century. (The key episode in that history is probably Lionel Trilling's failure to acknowledge the implicit sexuality of Fielding's first meeting with Aziz.[36]) Perhaps what is called for is a reading of the *propping* of the sexual valence of the incident on its apparent colonial (or anti-colonial) import. Readers of Laplanche will recognize my translation of his term *étayage*, a translation of Freud's *Anlehnung*, a "leaning" of the (sexualized) drive on the (functional) instinct. (*Propping* for *étayage* was the single translation that Laplanche resisted in our long and happy collaboration. John Fletcher, a major translator of Laplanche, has suggested—in a spirit of compromise?—that *propping* was an accurate translation of *étayage*, but *étayage* was an inaccurate translation of *Anlehnung*.[37]) It is hard to resist noting in this context that Forster's stud (in its sense of a device for fastening a collar in place) is virtually a synonym of English stay, from the same root as French *étai* as in *étayage*.

When (almost) all is said and done, the sexualized superimposability or resonance of what can be regarded as the culminating episode of Forster's first novel and the initial such episode of his final novel yields a chiasmus—or

---

36 Lionel Trilling, *E. M. Forster* (New York: New Directions, 1964).

37 See J. Mehlman, "*Verweile* doch! pour l'étayage" in *Colloque international de psychanalyse* (Paris: Presses Universes de France, 1994), pp. 79-86.

"hourglass"—of precisely the sort that Mauron, the dedicatee of *Aspects of the Novel,* had perfected in the discipline he called, somewhat awkwardly, *psychocritique.* Forster himself appears not to have discovered an egress from what he may have regarded as an impasse. *Where Angels Fear to Tread* dates from 1904; *A Passage to India,* fed to me as a freshman at Harvard in a context of unalloyed anti-colonialism, dates from 1924. The author died in 1971, which amounted to nearly a half century of avoiding the challenge of embarking on a new novel. Might Forster (after *A Passage to India*) have abandoned the novel as a *genre* as tellingly (and as enigmatically) as Racine abandoned tragedy (after *Phèdre*)? The British poet Tony Harrison once translated *Phèdre* in rhymed couplets, but transposed to the nineteenth century British Raj under the title *Phaedra Britannica.*[38] At a time that I was inclined to view Richard Wilbur's translation of *Phèdre* as a gold standard of the art, my great surprise as a teacher (of the Boston University translation seminar) was to find his achievement trumped by Harrison's *tour de force.* (I still recall Wilbur's reply to my question, when he came to the same seminar, of what he thought of Harrison's achievement: "a lot better than one would have hoped…"). Perhaps a study of Harrison's text would yield a commentary on the relation between the two authors—Racine, Forster— and their abandonment of their respective arts upon their having attained their zenith. But my effort here is to deepen all that might be at stake in the genius of Mauron and its inflection by what had been received in the form of Forster's dedication of *Aspects of the Novel* to him. Now the linkage of Racine, chiasmus, and "castration," as I already observed at the end of "Chiasmus," the central chapter of *Adventures in the French Trade,* came to Mauron, my teacher, via Forster's dedication, by way of his slightly disgruntled reading of Henry James' *The Ambassadors.* Which brings us to a different egress from James' novel in the form of an endgame played with the central essay of the volume (of "adventures in the French trade") preceding this one.

In 2010, the novelist Cynthia Ozick, whose work I had long admired, attempted an egress from *The Ambassadors* centred on a feminist inversion of James' plot. The action was centered in Paris, but during the post-World War II period of 1953. It stretches far west to California (where people are assumed to "know nothing") and far to the East (of Europe), where survivors of World

---

38 Tony Harrison, *Phaedra Britannica,* (London: Bellew Press, 1976).

War II are assumed to know too much, above all about death and inhumanity, from their experience during the war. The American population headed to Bohemian Paris aspired to being artists, poets. The population from the East consisted of refugees, mostly Jewish, and specifically Lili, a mangled, long suffering Romanian who is Ozick's version of James's Madame de Vionnet. She forms a couple with her version of Chad: an uncouth slob of a half-Jew named Julian with dreams of being an author of "clever little fables" with morals at the end so ambiguous that he calls them "immorals. (But already I am reminded that my readings during my year at Aix-en-Provence as a Fulbright scholar absorbing the lessons of Mauron were centered on a superimposition of Jules Laforgue's *Moralités légendaires*, brief works, in part translated by Ezra Pound and T. S. Eliot, that might be described in the terms used by Ozick to evoke Julian's aspirations.)

The central character of the novel is Bea, a high school English teacher in New York City and the "ambassador" charged by her obnoxious brother, Marvin, in California, with bringing Julian back home from Paris. Marvin, that is, corresponds to Mrs. Newsome of Massachusetts, even as Bea "without a life" corresponds to Lambert Strether… It is a circumstance that captures the gender inversion at the heart of what can be termed Ozick's chiasmus: a man commissions a woman in 2010 to do what a woman commissioned a man to do in 1903.

Marvin, the wealthy, self-hating Princetonian, however, does not exhaust Ozick's rewriting of Mrs. Newsome. For Mrs. Newsome is in fact split in two in the remake. Marvin is an odious Californian vulgarian, to be sure, a contemptuous nightmare of a brother. But he happens to live very near to Leo, a failed would-be musical genius, and Bea's nightmare of an ex-husband as well. Marvin and Leo are each fanatics of their own ego, and to that extent Californian narcissism incarnate. At the novel's eastern extreme, on the other hand, we find a world of "displaced persons," perhaps of displacement, the syntax of the unconscious itself. Silent Mrs Newsome in James, in sum, has been displaced by a failed musician who happens to be the mirror image of an unlikable brother, an individual whose specific form of cruelty is to make others pay the price for his musical failures.

The angry brother (Marvin) as musical failure (Leo), each fueling the ire of the other… The combination provides a clue of sorts to an important strand of Ozick's rewrite of Henry James, but appears to overlook the East

European motif, specifically the horror of the camps and the Holocaust. For if the attraction of Paris in James had everything to do with Madame de Vionnet and the refined poetry of intimacy, the fascination exercised by Lili, Ozick's version of Madame de Vionnet, is a function of the fascination exercised by horror. It is at this point that one is tempted to note the year of publication of *The Ambassadors*, 1903, for it was also the year of the legendary pogrom of Kishinev in Bessarabia. Kishinev was a small town in Moldova that knew a pogrom so violent that, despite its relatively small number of casualties (49 killed, 586 maimed), it came to figure in the Jewish imagination of the beginning of the twentieth century as a catastrophe comparable in status—or horror—to Auschwitz after World War II. (It was Kishinev, not the Dreyfus Affair, it has been said, which may have merited being viewed—as we, following Hannah Arendt, have suggested—as a dress rehearsal for the Holocaust. For it was Kishinev— the town where neighbors turned rapists—that knew the combination of familiarity and ferocity that may account for the true horror of the Holocaust.)

These lines are being written on a table with the naturalization papers of my maternal grandfather, Nathan Melnikoff, whom I never knew, in front of me.[39] He is identified as being born in Kishinev in 1880 The tragedy of Kishinev was written up by Chaim Nachman Bialik, the Hebrew national poet, as a record less of Cossacks killing Jews, than of Jewish males failing to protect their female relatives and companions. Such would be the laceration of Jewish male cowardice lamented in a monument of Hebrew national literature that might equally well have served as a monument to Jewish self-hatred of a sort not wholly alien to what we have observed in the preceding pages. Indeed, Bialik's "In the City of Killing" became known as the finest Jewish poem written since the Middle Ages.[40] And all the while it was an expression of contempt for what was taken to be the gender-marked moral deficiency of Jewish males.

And so we are led from what *Adventures in the French Trade* viewed as an originary scene of one man's relation to French literature, my own, through E. M. Forster's dedication of *Aspects of the Novel* to his friend (and my teacher),

---

39 Born in 1880 in Kishinev, Nathan Melnikoff arrived in New York from Southampton in 1903, the year of the pogrom, on a vessel bearing the same name--Saint Louis—as the boat of European refugees turned back by the American and Cuban governments in 1939.
40 Steven Zipperstein, *Pogrom and the Tilt of History* (New York: Norton, 2018), p. 107.

Charles Mauron, to a forgotten and more general context of European anti-semitism and self-hatred. The prospect is all the more surprising in that Henry James, whose novel, *The Ambassadors*, took on nodal (or seminal) significance in the process, had little to say about Jews other than his indifference to them. And yet the sequence of novels—or rereadings of *The Ambassadors*—mobilized in the process retained a skewed relation to the drama of the Jews. Thus our discussion of Blanchot, an endgame engaged under the rubric "Boston 1983" above, ended with a discussion of the emergence of the figure of the French intellectual during the Dreyfus Affair. And what finally remained of that series of transformations that took us from *The Ambassadors* to *Where Angels Fear to Tread*, and from there to Forster's final novel (and reputed masterpiece), *A Passage to India*, was a configuration—even after the central motif of sexual repression was introduced—quite intricately anticipatory of the Dreyfus Affair. The unjust trial of Dreyfus, the representative of a moral underclass, who was improbably supported by Picquart, the anti-semite and renegade who turned on his own army in the name of justice; the eventual collapse of the case for treason brought against Dreyfus, and the emergence of a Zionist (or Jewish nationalist) movement whose hero, according to Herzl, was the eponymous hero and victim of the Dreyfus Affair… This entire configuration appears transposed as the second half of *A Passage to India*: with the Indian Muslim Dr. Aziz, unjustly accused of rape, in the role of Dreyfus; the "renegade" Fielding in that of Picquart; the collapse of the case against Aziz during the deconstruction or nervous breakdown of the victim of the hallucinatory rape, Adela; Aziz emergent as the hero of a (future) Indian nationalist movement… And the fact that the nationalist movements of "Indianization" and/or Zionism should succeed long after the publication of *A Passage to India* in one case and the vindication of the Dreyfus Affair in the other yields an unexpectedly Judaic context for a major sequence of transformations in the history of the Anglo-American novel.[41]

And then, as though in confirmation of the gender flip informing the most elaborate recreation of James' novel, the plot of *The Ambassadors* emerged as fundamentally Judaic in Ozick's *Foreign Bodies*.[42] It was as though a full century after their initial emergence, James' classic novel of 1903 and the nightmare pogrom of Kishinev (also in 1903) began to bleed into each other.

---

41 E.M. Forster, *A Passage to India* (New York, Houghton Mifflin Harcourt), p. 296.
42 Cynthia Ozick, *Foreign Bodies*, (Boston: Houghton, Mifflin, Harcourt, 2010).

A solution? Ozick peers into the ghastly future as nightmare, following an expression of rage on the part of Bea-the-ambassador, realizing the full extent to which she has allowed Leo, her ex-husband, the failed composer (who seems always accompanied by Marvin, his narcissistic other, the insufferable brother) to make her pay the price for his own failures. "She splays the fingers of her left hand, curls the right into a knob; the left plunges into the bass; the fist crashed down on the treble. The sound was tremendous, the sound was august… It was the opening bars of the symphony he [Leo] was yet to write."[43] Her cacophony was sheer randomness, but simultaneously the expression of her rage at the lapse in being, the lapse in Bea-ing that her (unlived) life had been. Toward the end of the novel, Leo the failed musician sends his ex-wife the score of a Symphony he has written in B minor, i.e., in the imperative: Be Minor!, an order to never transcend the mediocre status he would condemn her to. The symphony turns out to be structured out of the cacophonous chord that we have heard Bea [Nightingale], in her rage, all but smash out on Leo's keyboard. It is to be called *The Nightingale's Thorn*, and what it punctures in its blindness is the narcissistic self-assurance of both Bea in her rage and Leo in his blindness. What binds the two together almost sacramentally in their nihilism, randomness, and incomprehension is what Kundera called emotional telepathy and Freud (with Laplanche) the unconscious in all its intensity.

Just before her novel ends, Ozick provides us with a snatch of movie music, composed by Leo specifically for a cartoon called *A Bargain for Betsy*. It is an exercise in *kitsch*, a Disneyish confection turning on a wicked wizard and the insalubrious jelly beans which he purveys to neighboring children instead of those healthful beans Betsy the beaver-lady supplies them with. In a word it is a remix of the Madwoman of Chaillot's manichean kitchen: half *schmaltz* (via Betsy), half *schmutz*. (via the wizard). Such would be the endgame that would follow on *La Folle de Chaillot*, the play that has supplied me with a medium for analysis since my engagement with Giraudoux in *Legacies: Of Anti-Semitism in France*.

But the subject of these pages is not specifically that of my volume (*Legacies*) on the fate, real or apparent, of an antipathy to Jews among French intellectuals once Hitler had in effect rendered it unavailable as an option in France. It is rather the afterlife of what had emerged as the skeletal unconscious

---

43 Ibid., p. 115.

of my life as a reading writer. After a survey of what appeared to insist without being acknowledged in a first memoir titled *Adventures in the French Trade: Fragments Toward a Life*—an antipathy to music, a relation to a brother as often *frerocious* (to use Pontalis' neologism) as conventionally fraternal, their connection to a lost French tradition of anti-semitism—the task has been to delve deeper into the four nodes, each structured by the figure of chiasmus, of the central chapter in that first memoir, and to reflect on their afterlife in the ten years since publication.

In reverse chronological order, then: my relation to the suppressed political past of Maurice Blanchot and the vindication of my work on it in Surya's recently published book; Laplanche's exemplary act of reading Freud's metapsychology as structured by an unperceived chiasmus, and the different chiasmus, between structure and speech act, in a second phase of Laplanche's ongoing investigation of Freud; Mauron's superimposition of Racine's tragedies in quest of what he called the seventeenth century master's unconscious, and Mauron's reinscription of that first exemplary reading in terms of Giraudoux's *oeuvre*; E. M. Forster's dedication to Mauron of his classic *Aspects of the Novel*, with its critique of the chiasmus or "hourglass" of Henry James' *The Ambassadors*, and its relation to Cynthia Ozick's rewriting of that very novel in a deeply Judaized context...

Such, in outline, is the turf I have been tilling over the last decade and such the concatenation of surprises (within surprises), a number of them anything but convenient, that has me willing to gather them with an eye to publication.

2

The Art of Being a Grandfather

Midst all the sentimental confusion surrounding one's acceding to grandfatherhood, it may be helpful to view the matter with a precision which, if not quite mathematical, is at least strikingly quantifiable. For acceding to grandfatherhood (or grandmotherhood, for that matter) is a matter, in most cases, of realizing that one will have enjoyed (or suffered) relations of genuine intensity with members of five successive generations. Simply put, they are the generations of one's grandparents, parents, siblings, children and grandchildren. Some, the great-grandparents among us, will have exceeded the number five, and others, "only children" deprived of siblings as we may be, may fall short of five, but as an ideal type, becoming a grandparent , a common destiny—given the state of medicine —among us, achieves fulfillment with the intuition of an altogether unexpected commerce of relations with members of a full five generations.

And what if what we call "the unconscious" were to entail an elaboration within just such a combination of intuition and unexpectedness? And to what extent does that last question shed light on the relatively obscure life's work of a scholar of matters French such as that of the author —and subject —of this book of "adventures" in the French trade? Let us begin then within that space—in an impassioned disagreement over the name to be assigned to the scholar's first-born child, his daughter Natalia. She might well not have been so named. For the fantasy of my mother, her grandmother, was that her destiny was to reincarnate (by bearing the name of) my recently deceased (and much beloved) grandmother, Anna. When the feud subsided, it was the partisans of a quasi- Argentine future named Natalia who had won the day. Tears were no doubt shed on behalf of Anna and the past, and a very bright future could begin.

It was not until several years later that Alicia, I believe, made the casual observation that my maternal grandfather (i.e., Anna's husband), who had died in the 1920s at a rather young age and whom I had never known, was named Nathan. And that "Natalia" is more than arguably a feminization of "Nathan." The argument over Natalia's name, that is, was rooted in a failure to perceive the buried Russian—or, more specifically, Judeo-Bessarabian—core of her first name.

But I don't believe I would have had "Nathan" in mind had it not been for my grandfather's "declaration of intention," signed on October 31, 1906, in an application to the Bureau of Immigration and Naturalization for citizenship in the United States. That document was eventually consigned to cyberspace, from which it was ultimately plucked and forwarded to me by my cyber-savvy son Ezra. Now the most acutely charged aspect of that declaration, in retrospect, was the reporting of Nathan Melnikoff's place of birth, which was the town of Kishinev, the largest city (with a population of 110,000) of the Russian rump state of Moldova. For Kishinev was the town whose anti-semitic violence culminated in the introduction of the Russian word *pogrom* into the conventional vocabularies of a variety of European languages.[1] And the specificity of the violence of Kishinev, what made it a watchword, before World War II, comparable in its dire extremity to what Auschwitz would later become after the war, was less the number of murders it encompassed than the extent of the violence done to women and, above all, of the failure of the males of Kishinev to defend their womenfolk.

It was that failure of virility, the apparent cowardice that saw the men of Kishinev back away from the challenge of defending their women, that became the idiosyncratic focus of the most noted poem, "In the City of the Slaughter," of the Hebrew national poet, Chaim Nachman Bialik. And this in turn suggests that between literature and a kind of self-lacerating Hebraic equivalent of what Freud called "primary masochism," there might be a kind of parity.

Literature, then, as a meditation on a self-inflicted wound to be cul-

---

1 See Steven Zipperstein, *Pogrom: Kishinev and the Tilt of History* (New York: Norton, 2018).

tivated… Or perhaps as an attempt to confront and then answer the question tearfully asked over the phone by the mother of the protagonist of Philip Roth's seminal novel, *The Ghost Writer.* "Could it be you are an anti-semite?" And then one recalls that that protagonist, neurotic scion of the Zuckerman clan, is (first) named "Nathan". And that *The Ghost Writer* relates a fantasied love affair between Nathan and that heroine of post-Holocaust fiction, Anne Frank. But if Philip Roth could best imagine himself as the fantasied love affair between a "Nathan" and an "Anne" (Frank), it was because the flawed love of a Nathan (Melnikoff) for an Anna was a letter of sorts, sent from the depths of just what anonymity?, into what we believe to be the future.

That model of a life as an anonymously sent letter of unknown author appears as a loan from an image at the beginning of "Chiasmus," the central chapter of *Adventures in the French Trade: Fragments Toward a Life.* It is an image borrowed from Paul Morand and culminates with the suggestion that the readerly task might be to discover the postmarks on the envelope of the letter a life—as a (reading) writer —will have been. And that image found its point of insistence, but moving in an other direction, years later when I received, via e-mail, a drawing by my six year old grand-daughter, then spending a semester (with her mother Natalia, who was then teaching a course for the New School) in France. The picture was of a carefully disarticulated French Tricolour, its vertical stripes—left to right —of blue, white, and red being replaced by horizontal stripes—top to bottom—of red, white, and blue. Just above that apparent (and imperfect) postmark (from the future to the past), moreover, the words "Boston Paris" were featured. And still more striking was the single word "BYE," which might be read as a farewell (before it even begins) to either the addressee of its message or the dimension of reference (message, or even meaning) itself. BYE as an essential evanescence of content, that is, is much like that of the legendary purloined letter expropriated by Lacan from Poe and which I translated as part of a legendary issue of *Yale French Studies* titled *French Freud.*

And then that one final addendum or supplement to the postmark: the misspelling of the phrase "Alicia too," as if to acknowledge, model grand-daughter that she was and is, that grandfathers were fine, but the last word on and in this business of grand-parenting must rightfully be reserved for a grandmother.

The motif of the letter, purloined or not, sent from the future to the past, figured as well in my first volume of memoirs, *Adventures in the French*

Trade, but sent from the past to a certain future, as was the case for E. M. Forster's dedication of his classic *Aspects of the Novel* (1927) to Charles Mauron. Charles Mauron was associated in that first volume with a technique of textual superimposition and found himself to be a locus of repetition invested in the figure of chiasmus as it structured Forster's reading of Henry James' novel of 1903, *The Ambassadors*. And Forster's critique of the elaborately structured novel of James, said to be suitable for Racinian tragedy (but not for a European novel), seemed to open the path to Mauron's delineation of a Racinian unconscious and to everything that Freud might bring to the art of reading.

Mauron, among other things, had served as mayor of the Provençal town of Saint-Rémy, a place nearby to Aix-en-Provence, which, for that very reason, figured as one of the postmarks of the letter of my life as a reader. And that was, no doubt, why Natalia and her brood chose to surprise me with her visit to one of the stations construable as a node of her father's unconscious. Did the message from Lucy to her grandfather, future to past, encompass the message from E.M. Forster to Charles Mauron, past to future, or was it the reverse? The jury may have been out on that question, but one sign of its pertinence was the photo I received during the spring of 2018. Mauron, as mentioned, had been mayor of Saint-Rémy de Provence. It was for that reason that the town ended up naming a street after him—the Avenue Charles Mauron, which was the destination of a touching pilgrimage in the spring of 2018. According to Toby, Lucy's elder brother, the trip to what he called "the Avenue"—since the grandeur of what was more, after all, than a mere "street," meant more to him than the alleged achievement or genius of Mauron—was inspired by sheer affection for his grandfather.

The photograph from Saint-Rémy was of the assembled family of my daughter and son-in-law beneath the street sign of "Avenue Charles Mauron." It raises the question, at least in this reader's mind, of what, then, it might mean to inscribe an—or *the*—experience of French literature within the dialogue of a Jew and his grandchildren. Readers of these pages may encounter later on two photographs e-mailed back to Boston from what seemed to be a random seaside resort in Normandy. Did Natalia know that Cabourg, the resort, was the site of much of the action of Proust's masterwork, *A la recherche du temps perdu*, where it bears the name "Balbec"? The photos showed Lucy and Toby enjoying the splendor of the lobby of the Grand Hôtel de Cabourg. But there is another mis-

sive from Cabourg which captures the core of Proust's novel with such concision as to be worth figuring as a submission in the legendary contest to come up with the shortest summary of Proust's novel extant. It was sent on August 19, 1916, by Emile Durkheim, founder of the science of sociology, to his nephew, Marcel Mauss. It began, that is, with the words *Cher Marcel...* In it Durkheim relates to Mauss the experience of arriving on the beach at Cabourg, only to find that it is unpleasantly over-run (*encombrée*) with "sémites de tout sexe."

Now if Cabourg/Balbec is the site of a good half of the action of Proust's novel, the other half seems generated in—or *en*—Combray (a homonym of Durkheim's past participle *encombrée* in the passage cited). And the notion of "Semites of every sex," for all its apparent comedy, manages to capture the elements of the longest simile of Proust's novel, whose two components are what he calls the "accursed races" of Jews and sexual "inverts." In brief, we are confronted with another case of Jewish self-contempt transmitted unconsciously through the internal correspondence between generations of a Jewish family. And to the extent that Lévi-Strauss ascribed to Mauss the invention of a usable concept of the "unconscious;" that that concept might also be understood as a version of the "floating signifier;" and that the homophony between *encombrée* and *en-Combray* offers just such a version of the signifier afloat, the encounter of Durkheim and Mauss offers a superlative instance of what might be at stake in a structural understanding of the unconscious.

And every maneuver seems to mediate a bout of Jewish self-disdain. Such is the case in the novel of Proust, to be sure,[2] but also in what transpires between "Nathan" and "Anne" in Philip Roth's *The Ghost Writer* as well. But, as if by duplication, Nathan's romancing of Anne, it turns out, transmits to a life, that of my forebearers, the Kishinev dynamic: a tragedy less of Nathan or Anna's death, as might be expected (and regretted) in the case of a pogrom, than of a failure to come to the aid of a violated woman. Expand the field beyond literature—i.e, Proust's masterpiece—itself to that of the psyche—or at least of my psyche—and one zeroes in on the psychoanalyst Jean Laplanche and his appreciation, if such be the word, of what he called, after a reading of my *Adventures in the French Trade*, my "amours antisémites."

The advantage accruing to our reading relates to the resurgence of an awareness of the episode of the Kishinev pogrom behind that of the episode that Hannah Arendt would refer to as a dress rehearsal for the Holocaust, the Dreyfus Affair. But the Dreyfus Affair would resurface in my own life in a context of grandpaternal pathos, almost as though the events of Kishinev, the Bessarabian birthplace of my grandfather, would transmit their grandfatherly essence to the eminently Gallic adventure—of Dreyfus—which had repressed them.

**

That development can be summarized in terms of two centenary celebrations held at the Cardozo Law School, gatherings at which I happen to have spoken, and, more tellingly, at which the interests of the arch-victim of an anti-semitic campagn in Europe happened to be represented by a grandson of that same victim. On the occasion of the centenary of the Dreyfus Affair, which occurred in 1994, a full hundred years after the court martial and exile to Devil's Island of Alfred Dreyfus, my talk concerned Hannah Arendt's proposition that the Affair might be regarded as a "foregleam" or "dress rehearsal" of what would later be called the Holocaust, but more remarkably still as what might be regarded as a kind of second act in a tragedy whose initial episode (or first act) was the catastrophic fiasco of the French failure to build the Panama Canal.

---

2 Whence the aptness of Serge Doubrovsky's dedication to me of a copy of his quasi-Proustian *roman à clef Un amour de soi* (Paris: Hachette, 1982): thanking me for my *Legacies of Anti-Semitism in France*, and then characterizing his riff on Proust as a *"règlement de comptes sado-maso-sémite."*

The Dreyfus grandson in New York, meanwhile, was Charles, who had a distinct recollection of Alfred Dreyfus during the 1930s and his hesitation, after his pardon, to discuss the events of his victimization. The sole episode which the Captain seemed never to have assimilated, neutralized or overcome, according to Charles Dreyfus, the grandson who had graduated from Stuyvesant High School in New York, related to the revelation during the (second) Rennes trial that General Boisdeffre, who pretended, during the initial court martial, to be an ally of Alfred Dreyfus, revealed himself to be an architect of the frame-up of Dreyfus. It was the most ineradicable (i.e., crushing) incident in the Dreyfus Affair for that Affair's protagonist, but also the event that so affected me during the year I spent translating Bredin's history of the Affair that I felt—such were my tears—compelled to set aside my efforts as a translator.

The second centenary at Cardozo was of the Beilis trial of 1913. Accused of a blood libel, the "Russian Dreyfus," as he was called, was prosecuted for raping and murdering a young boy. And then, the weakness of the prosecution's case having been admitted, an attempt was made to get him to quash the affair by accepting a pardon. He refused lest the concomitant admission of guilt provoke a series of pogroms in Kiev. It was a position further grounded in a variety of promises by wealthy Jews that they would support Beilis lavishly out of a will to compensate him for the suffering he endured, the principal problem being that such compensation ended up not being forthcoming.

The Cardozo colloquium of 2014 featured the participation of Beilis' grandson, Jay, who was particularly eloquent on what he called the plagiarism of Beilis's memoir by the novelist Bernard Malamud in his prize-winning novel *The Fixer*. Indeed the stance of Jay Beilis consisted of viewing *The Fixer* as a further stripping of what was rightfully his grandfather's, lamentable *schnorrer* that he was. But it would be important to specify that if the curse of the Beilis clan was to be the legacy of a world-class *schnorrer*, the curse of the Dreyfus clan was to be the legacy of a world-class *schlemiel*—to wit, the Captain's willingness to place his trust in Boisdeffre, a principal architect of his suffering.

In sum, the two grandchildren of the two world-class victims of anti-semitism, Dreyfus the *schlemiel* and Beilis the *schnorrer*, seemed to be enacting a particularly painful observation of Hannah Arendt: "when he [the Jew] tried to stop the pariah from being a *schlemiel*, when he sought to give him a political significance, he encountered only the *schnorrer...*"[3] Such would be the Jewish self-hatred we have seen in counterpoint to our argument on aesthetic pain. We might call it feminist, coming as it does from Hannah Arendt, but it should not be forgotten that Malamud himself is embodied in *The Ghost Writer* by the character of the almost Jamesian novelist E. I Lonoff, protagonist of Roth's novel.

Which brings us back from the grandchildren whose grandfather the author of these pages is to the grandfather whose posthumous grandchild he would eventually be, the man whose application for American residence just after the Kishinev pogrom might serve to define the contours of the space within which he would write and be written. A historian of the pogrom has insisted on the specific vulnerability or pain that served as a defining feature of the Jewish world of the Kishinev disgrace. Bialik, the Hebrew national poet, has invoked such aspects of that catastrophe in terms of the "half-demented" God who visited the violation of the women of Kishinev on their men, shuddering in shame as they did at their inability (or refusal?) to intervene in any way to forestall their humiliation. Such was the most striking feature of Hebrew literature—in Bialik's "In the City of the Slaughter," the "most influential Jewish poem" since the Middle Ages—as it offered up its revulsion at Jewish humiliation or passivity insofar as it was to become a mainstay of the Hebrew academic canon. The eccentricity of that central configuration was such that Bialik, in a letter to Joseph Klausner, ended up associating it with an ordeal of his own: a repeated beating on his buttocks in an outhouse by a cousin in Russia during his childhood.[4] Such would be the psychosocial nucleus in which Israeli academia was prepared to locate what the historian S. Zipperstein has characterized as something of its centerpiece. But that development, in turn, would guide us into its intersection with Freud's's crucial treatment of what he called the "economic problem of masochism," specifically in his disarticulation of the fantasy "A Child Is Being Beaten." But that link turns out to mesh with one of the key moments in the history of speculative reading, the analysis of "A Child Is Being Beaten" just prior to the emergence of the "death drive" (or "death instinct" or "anti-instinct") in Laplanche's *Vie et mort en psychanalyse*, a work whose crucial situation in the history of reading is one of the foci of the cen-

---

3 "The Jew as a Pariah" in Hannah Arendt, *The Jewish* Writings (New York: Schocken, 2007), p. 285.
4 Zipperstein, p. 125.

terpiece of *Adventures in the French Trade: Fragments Toward a Life*, the chapter called "Chiasmus."

But if what psychoanalysis calls primary masochism (or, why not? Jewish self-hatred) might end up being one of the ends or vicissitudes of the fate of the Jews (as much as of reading itself), that intersection receives an additional "foundation," to use a tag out of Laplanche's recent work, as well. For it turns out that one of the key inspirations of Bessarabian anti-semitism, the journalist Pavel Krushevan, was in some respects a figure quite similar to France's Edouard Drumont: a literary traditionalist and, simultaneously, a particularly rabid populist journalist. It was Drumont's polemical rag, *La libre parole*, that was said to have given us the Dreyfus Affair. But it was Krushevan's prose in *Bessarabetz* at the beginning of the century which, according to one historian, "managed to push the Dreyfus Affair to the margins."[5] But Krushevan, in addition to an early version of *The Protocols of the Elders of Zion*, left behind a legacy in prose, a memoir or archive of sorts that he bestowed on a journalist associate who, in turn, found himself fleeing Moldova once the Soviet Union collapsed. His name was Mikhail Khazin and he escaped from Russia in old age only to settle in Brookline, Massachusetts, not far from what would be the home of the author of these pages. The elements of a reading begin to be assembled: the Kishinev disgrace of 1903, a quintessential manifestation of anti-Jewish violence, a scandal linked more to the passivity of Jewish males than to the brutality of Russian cossacks, a literature organized—via Bialik's poem—around sexual trauma, "a child being beaten," the title of a key Freudian text, an episode in the most revealing of readings, that visited, with its lessons, by way of Laplanche in a book I translated almost fifty years ago… And they all end up so improbably close to Brookline's most famous monument, Fenway Park, that not only is Mikhail Khazin, the Moldovan archivist, escaping Russia with his documents, queried as to whether or not he had ever been there, but when confronted with that query, he could only reply that he did not know what his interlocutor was talking about…

The year 1903 was not only that of the Kishinev pogrom and the plague of violent antisemitism that followed in its wake. It was also the year of Henry James' *The Ambassadors* and the variety of novels which *it* trailed in its

---

5 Ibid., p. 11.

wake. E. M. Forster was intermittently distressed by *The Ambassadors*, and the absence of any trace of mutiny or rebelliousness on the part of James' characters seemed to him, in *Aspects of the Novel*, which he dedicated to Charles Mauron in 1927, a clearcut deficiency. That did not, however, prevent Forster, in his first novel, *Where Angels Fear to Tread*, from following the plot of *The Ambassadors*—with its failed attempt to bring back a British family member gone astray on the Continent—in some detail. Let us retain for its emblematic value the excruciating stalking by an Italian, Gino, of Philip Herriton, the British protagonist, whose broken arm is twisted in its socket by Gino. In its unmatched (and patently sexualized) intensity, it marks a kind of culmination or turning point of the first of Forster's novels. And then consider the *last* of Forster's novels, *A Passage to India*, or rather the possibility of superimposing that last of his novels on the first. The Indian peninsula replaces the Italian peninsula, as the narrator observes, and a failed relation of unmatched intensity between the Englishman Fielding and the Indian Aziz is unfurled. More specifically, the emotional core of Forster's final novel at its inception focuses on Aziz's gift of a missing collar stud to be inserted (at a certain risk!) in the rear hole of his shirt collar. This risky insertion of stud-in-collar marks the beginning of the culminating erotic relationship in Forster's fiction. Which means that the final erotic relation, however flawed, in Forster's first work of fiction is rigorously superimposable on the intitial erotic episode in Forster's culminating work of fiction. Moreover the form taken by that superimposition is that of a reverse-return, chiasmus, or what has been called by Forster himself, in *Aspects of the Novel*, an hour-glass. And this entire development would seem to be born of the critical perceptiveness of Charles Mauron, whose plunge into the world of superimpositions and reverse-returns, no less than his role as dedicatee of Forster's *Aspects of the Novel*, underwrite what is being proposed in these pages.

And then, as if to press the point to a certain limit, we are confronted with *Foreign Bodies*, Cynthia Ozick's rewriting (in 2010) of *The Ambassadors*. Having observed the puncture of an idyllic French landscape (or narcissistic bubble) by the pink point of a parasol in the penultimate chapter of the James novel;[6] having pierced that imaginary idyll with its violently deflationary thrust;

---

6 Henry James, *The Ambassadors* (New York: Norton, 1964), p. 309: "What he saw was exactly the right thing—a boat advancing round the bend and containing a man who held the paddles and a lady, at the stern, with a pink parasol."

and having done so even as a work of music, *The Nightingale's Thorn*, in *Foreign Bodies*, would serve to splay the world of the idyll with the dissonance of its devil's interval, the structure within which I have come to find myself reading in recent years approaches completion. At the beginning, Kishinev and the Bessarabian violence of 1903... At the end, a recasting by Ozick of *The Ambassadors*, James' novel of that same year... In between—and in the orbit of the problematically truncated careers of one great author (Racine) or another (Forster), the pursuit of a technique of textual superimposition and all that it shares with what Freud cast as a technique of "free association" have issued in an articulation of the categories of discovery and pain to which a number of the developments in these pages, beginning with "Endgames," its initial title, are intended to make a contribution.

3

The Dreyfus Affair:
Dress Rehearsal or Second Act?

There is a quip occasionally repeated by historians that provides a some-what unsettling entry into the subject of the Dreyfus Affair. If, the line goes, in 1925, someone had said that within twenty years, close to six million Jews would be slaughtered in Europe, the most plausible response, after initial gasps of dis-belief, might well have been to reply: "Ah the French, will they actually go that far!" It is the anti-Semitic riots, the virtual pogroms taking place in every major French city in 1898 that no doubt underlies the sinister joke and explains the force, indeed the horrific aptness, of the punchline, however historically errone-ous it might have turned out to be. To which one might add everything implicit in the subtitle given by the Israeli scholar Zeev Sternhell to his important work about political thought in France in the years surrounding the Dreyfus Affair. That subtitle, it may be recalled, was not the "origins of French fascism," but the "French origins of fascism."[1]

The nightmare of twentieth century Europe viewed as an offshoot of the turmoil of nineteenth century Paris? Such was, of course, the intuition behind Walter Benjamin's unfinished Arcades Project, but such as well was the thought behind his friend Hannah Arendt's take on the Dreyfus Affair as a "huge dress rehearsal" for the genocide perpetrated by the Nazi regime. Given the post-

---

1 Zeev Sternhell, *La Droite révolutionnaire: Les origines françaises du fascisme* (Paris: Seuil, 1978).

humous publication of an important collection of texts by Arendt (*The Jewish Writings*), I propose to take a look at the principal articulations of Arendt's reading of the Affair as "foregleam" of the Holocaust, one which simultaneously offers a kind of anticipation of her reading of the Nazi period in her book on the Eichmann trial, *The Banality of Evil*.[2]

My sense is that Arendt's vision of the Affair (like her vision of the Holocaust) is dictated by a fundamental allergy to the genre of melodrama. Melodrama, being the sentimental struggle of the forces of good against the forces of evil, is inherently manipulative of its audience. (And it was precisely a reaction against such manipulation by the Dreyfusards that drove the poet Valéry, or so he tells us, to contribute his gift, "not without reflection," to the anti-Dreyfusard cause.[3]) Now the *other* of melodrama, the genre to which it is classically opposed, is tragedy, defined by Hegel as a conflict in which both sides are right.[4] (Thus the Arendtian Alain Finkielkraut on the conflict in the Middle East as tragedy.) In the case of the Dreyfus Affair (but also the Holocaust), the anti-Semites were so obviously in the wrong that there could be no question of invoking tragedy (in which both sides are in the right). The result is that Arendt's way of avoiding melodrama is to carve out a story (or a genre) in which both sides are *wrong*.

It is not clear that we have a name for such a genre, perhaps satire, but I suspect the person who was most alive to its limitations was Gershom Scholem, in his letter of June 23, 1963 to Arendt on the tone of *The Banality of Evil*.[5] The term he used was the English word *flippancy*, a "frequently malicious, almost sneering tone" that might flare up in a phrase such as "the Jewish *Führer* Leo Baeck," and more generally in Arendt's thesis that what made the Nazi genocide possible was not that the Jews had failed to organize, but that they *were* organized, and that their leadership, "almost without exception, cooperated in one

---

2 Hannah Arendt, *The Jewish Writings* (New York: Schocken, 2007).
3 Michel Jarrety, *Paul Valéry* (Paris: Fayard, 2008), pp. 239—255.
4 See "Hegel's Interpretation of *Antigone* in *Encyclopaedia Britannica Online* (April 1999): "The nuclear Greek tragedy for Hegel is, understandably, Sophocles' ***Antigone***, with its conflict between the valid claims of conscience (Antigone's obligation to give her brother a suitable burial) and law (King Creon's edict that enemies of the state should not be allowed burial). The two claims represent what Hegel regards as essentially concordant ethical claims."
5 Gershom Scholem, *On Jews and Judaism in Crisis* (New York: Schocken, 1976), p. 302.

48

way or another, for one reason or another, with the Nazis."[6] Let us see how that posture on Arendt's part, that absence of what Scholem called "Ahavat Yisrael," love of Israel, manifested itself in her reading of the Dreyfus Affair. It would take us from the characterization of Dreyfus as a *parvenu*, which for Arendt was the ultimate putdown, to the mocking description of the Dreyfus family, who, in "trying to save an innocent man," "employed the very methods [opening up their wallets, hiring a publicist] usually adopted in the case of a guilty one," and all the way to a quotation from Bernard Lazare to the effect that for the three dozen or so [Jews] in France who were ready to defend one of their martyred brethren you could find some thousands ready to stand guard over Devil's Island, alongside the most rabid patriots of the country."[7] Arendt even goes so far as to quote André Foucault in 1938, characterizing the contempt of the Dreyfus family for unassimilated eastern Jewry: "The Dreyfuses of 1894? Why they were anti-semites!"[8]

Here then, in Arendt's castigation of the guilty victims of the Dreyfus Affair, is a "foregleam" of the complicitous victims of the Nazi genocide in *The Banality of Evil*. Of course, to make the link between the Affair and the Holocaust stick, Arendt had to take matters out of the courtroom and see things as fundamentally political. And here her attention alights on Jules Guérin, the leader of the Ligue antisémitique and the stager of an unsuccessful coup d'état against the republic in February 1899. Jules Guérin, we are all but told, would resurface as Hitler: "The Jules Guérins had to wait nearly forty years before the atmosphere was ripe again for quasi-military storm troops."[9] As the vital link between the Affair and the Holocaust, Guérin fascinated Arendt. He is described as "the most modern figure" of the anti- Dreyfusards, the stylishly *louche* denizen of the underworld in whom "high society found its first criminal

---

6 Hannah Arendt, *The Origins of Totalitarianism* (New York: Harcourt Brace Jovanovich, 1973), p. 72.

7 Ibid., pp. 91, 105, 117.

8 Ibid., p. 103.
Oddly enough, the characterization applies perfectly to Arendt's exemplary Jewish intellectual, Bernard Lazare, who was capable of writing, before the Affair: "it would suffice for our anti-semites, having at last attained justice, to become anti-Jews instead. They could be sure of having many an anti-Israelite with them on such a day."

9 Arendt, ibid., p. 94.

hero."[10] Jules Guérin as prototype, then. His legendary headquarters, on the rue de Chabrol, described by our author as the "first of the 'Brown Houses." Except for the fact that for any reader of Marx, the surprise is that Guérin's attempted coup seems less a prototype than a farcically weak echo of the (already farcical) Eighteenth Brumaire of Louis Bonaparte. Guérin, that is, may have been a dress rehearsal, a *répétition générale*, for Nazism, but he represented no less a *repetition* of Marx's script for Louis Bonaparte's coup of December 2, 1851. One may recall that for Marx the specificity of what happened in France in 1851 was that the dialectic of class struggle between bourgeoisie and proletariat came to a sinister standstill as the *lumpenproletariat*, the drop-outs of the class struggle, gathered around the eminently sinister figure of Louis Bonaparte and pushed through his imperial coup.[11] To the shock of Marx, French history, which should have flushed away the drop-outs of the class struggle, began to resemble nothing so much as a latrine backing up. Here now is Hannah Arendt on Guérin's counterpart to the *lumpen* cohort of Napoleon III: "The mob is primarily a group in which the residue of all classes" are to be found."[12] (107) Marx's *lumpen* drop-outs; Arendt's residues… In genuine revolutions, she tells us, the people fight for "true representation." With the "residues," representation is beside the point. And just as Arendt's anti-Dreyfusard intelligentsia was said (not entirely accurately) to have but recently emerged from "a ruinous and decadent cult of aestheticism," Louis Bonaparte's lumpen-proletariat was dubbed by Marx "the whole amorphous disintegrated mass of flotsom and jetsom the French call *la bohème*."[13] Finally, just as, for Arendt, bourgeois society, "in its adulation of Guérin," "had broken for good with its own standards," so for Marx, had the bourgeoisie, in rallying to Louis Bonaparte, shown a willingness to sacrifice its own values (free speech, etc) in order to protect its economic privileges.

In brief, for all her insistence on Tocqueville at the beginning of her long essay on anti-Semitism in *The Origins of Totalitarianism*, Arendt, in her unforgettable treatment of the Dreyfus Affair, seems to be harking back to Marx's masterpiece, *The Eighteenth Brumaire of Louis Bonaparte*.

---

10 Ibid, p. 111.
11 See my *Revolution and Repetition: Marx/Hugo/Balzac* (Berkeley: University of California Press, 1977).
12 Arendt, Ibid., p. 107.
13 See *Revolution and Repetition*, p. 13.

Unforgettable? I would like to turn now to what strikes me as the most remarkable section of her discussion and which nonetheless goes unmentioned in the historical critiques of her reading of the Affair by both Michael Marrus and Pierre Birnbaum. It concerns the notion that the Dreyfus Affair begins "not with the arrest of a Jewish staff officer but with the Panama scandal."[14] For it is the notion that the Affair, before being a "dress rehearsal" for the tragedy of the Holocaust, was the second act of a two-act drama that begins with Panama that gives Arendt's version of the Affair its particular pungency.

In a word, the Panama fiasco was France's Big Dig in the late nineteenth century—one of those French catastrophes, a bit like World War II, that would be taken up and brought to successful completion by the Americans. It was, Arendt writes, a "colossal racket," replete with payoffs and bribes, and in which French citizens were invited to invest, with the result that some half-million middle-class Frenchmen ended up in financial ruin.[15] Now the key element relating to the Dreyfus Affair concerned the two principal intermediaries charged with bribing members of parliament, both of them Jewish, Jacques de Reinach and Cornelius Herz. Eventually Herz began blackmailing Reinach, who committed suicide in 1892, but not before—and this is crucial--handing over a list of those he had bribed to Edouard Drumont, the anti-semitic leader, muckraker, and editor of *La Libre Parole*, on condition that he (Drumont), cover up for Reinach personally. With remarkable cunning Drumont released the names of the corrupt parliamentarians bit by bit, thereby building suspense—as well as the readership (and the influence) of his newspaper, which was principally an anti-Semitic rag.

Now the Dreyfus Affair begins within the context of the Panama racket, a racket attributed largely to the Jews, even though there were no Jewish parliamentarians on Reinach's list. In Arendt's formulations, the Jews were but "parasites" on a thoroughly "corrupt body," the French state, and thus available for scapegoating.[16] Herz, in Bernanos's phrase, was a "parasite on a parasite" (Reinach). Reinach, that is, was bleeding France, and Herz was bleeding Reinach. Think of the Leonard Bernstein waltz from *Candide*.

---

14 Arendt, p. 95.
15 Ibid., p. 95.
16 Ibid., p.99.

What's the use?
What's the use
Of dishonest endeavor
And being so clever?
It's wrong,
Oh, so wrong!
If you just have to pass it along.[17]

Now, the image of Jacques de Reinach at the center of the physical and ethical swamp of Panama was striking. We know that Jacques de Reinach's closest associate, the man who discovered his corpse, was his nephew, Joseph, the future Dreyfusard leader. As for Herz, who appears to have been a world class swindler, a friend of Thomas Edison and a man of genuine talent, who even served a stint as a physician on the staff of Mount Sinai Hospital in New York (until it was determined that his alleged graduation from the University of Paris was fictitious), he eventually escaped Paris for England, where he declared himself too ill to return to France.[18] In an interview unmentioned by Arendt, he declared that the reason he refused to return to France was that he had been accused of treason in the Chamber, which meant that he could be tried behind closed doors and sent to Devil's Island.[19] The interview with Herz was published in February 1893, in the New York Herald, the year before the Dreyfus court martial. At which point, enter Captain Dreyfus, with all his love of France, all of his ideals, in the role of the *schlemiel.* One last item: Herz's friend, protégé, and publicist was Georges Clemenceau, the future publisher of "J'accuse" and Arendt's choice for the role of true hero of the Dreyfus Affair.

In sum, once one switches the perspective from dress rehearsal to second act, an entirely different Affair emerges. The only thing comparable I can think of is something that happens in the Bible. Open up the book of Exodus and one finds the horrific enslavement of the Jews; but if one goes back a few pages to the end of Genesis, one finds a description of the enslavement of the Egyptian feudal class through the wiles of Joseph, the court Jew, in the employ

---

17 Leonard Bernstein, Lillian Helman, Richard Wilbur, *Candide,* 1956.
18 David McCullough, *Path Between the Seas: The Creation of the Panama Canal 1870- 1914* (New York: Simon and Schuster, 1977), p. 214.
19 Ibid., p. 229.

of Pharaoh, during the years of famine… It is precisely the relationship between the Dreyfus Affair and the Panama scandal.

Or put it this way. The Canadian writer Mavis Gallant once commented that she had been living for years in France, but it was not until she read a history of the Dreyfus Affair that things became clear to her. It was, she noted, as though up until then she had been watching television with the sound turned off. Presumably, what she heard were the cries of "Death to the Jews" during the riots of 1898. But there is a telling variant to that sound track: according to Georges Bernanos, Drumont's self- proclaimed disciple and a principle source for Arendt, the "patriotic" bands of Jules Guérin would make their way, during the Affair, down the rue Montmartre to the offices of *L'Aurore*, the paper where "J'Accuse!" was published. The refrain they chanted made no mention of Jews, It was "Pa-na-ma! Pa-na-ma!"[20]

To summarize, the legacy of the Affair may have been the Holocaust, but the Affair itself was a legacy of the Panama scandal. And from the point of view of Drumont and the professional anti-Semites, it was Panama, not Dreyfus, that offered the perfect storm. For in the Dreyfus Affair they would be forced to deal with an innocent scapegoat whereas in the Panama case, they had the luxury of dealing with not one but two *guilty* scapegoats (Reinach and Herz).

Or to phrase things in comparative terms, there were two reactions to the French failure to build the Panama Canal. The American reaction was… to build the Panama Canal. The French reaction was to give us the Dreyfus Affair.

To have salvaged the refrain of Pa-na-ma, implicit in the other more familiar, more ghastly refrain (Death to the Jews!), to have imagined the dress rehearsal (for the Holocaust) as a kind of second act (after Panama), is to unsettle our melodramatic certainties about the morality play of the Affair and to endow it with a measure of credibility it would perhaps not otherwise have. Such was the contribution of the "egregious Hannah Arendt," as Isaiah Berlin called her, to our understanding of the Affair, and such is our debt to her for it.

---

20 Georges Bernanaos, *La Grande Peur des bien-pensants* (Paris: Livre de poche, 1931), p. 293.

4

Dreyfus/Beilis/History/Literature: Notes Toward a Memoir

"When he tried to stop the pariah from being a *schlemiel,*
when he sought to give him a political significance,
he encountered only the *schnorrer…*"
Hannah Arendt, "The Jew as Pariah: A Hidden Tradition"

Some years ago, thanks to the initiative of Richard Weisberg, I found myself at the Cardozo School of Law, where I was part of a colloquium celebrating (or commemorating) one of a sequence of centenaries of the Dreyfus Affair, and featuring as keynote speaker none other than Dreyfus's grandson, Charles (who was well into his eighties at the time). It was a particularly moving experience. These remarks have as their occasion a second visit to Cardozo for a colloquium intended to commemorate the centenary of the Beilis Affair, conducted with the collaboration of Mendel Beilis' grandson Jay. And I suspect that the choice of my four-part title—Dreyfus/Beilis/History/Literature—was in part dictated by the congruence of those two sequences, those two Affairs. But before delving into what my title is intended to convey, allow me to state what I found most moving, most revealing, in that earlier encounter with the grandson of a world-class victim of anti-Semitism, Captain Alfred Dreyfus. In fact, I am far more familiar with the Dreyfus than with the Beilis Affair, and my familiarity stems largely from the fact that forty years ago I translated what many still regard as this generation's exemplary history of the sequence, Jean-Denis Bredin's *The Affair*.[1] Now concerning that translation, I recall—indelibly—that while executing it I at one point found the situation of Dreyfus so excruciating that I broke into tears and had to set aside the translation. But curiously, by the time I arrived at Cardozo for the Dreyfus colloquium, although I recalled that traumatic interruption of my translation, I could not remember (had I repressed it?) the episode that I found so excruciating and that had been the cause of that interruption. And that is where the victim's grandson cast his particular illumination. For on being asked whether the Captain—whom Charles had known, and who had died in 1934, a year after Beilis—ever talked with the family about his ordeal, he answered that the only memory that the Captain himself seemed never to have gotten over related to General Boisdeffre, the head of the Army General Staff. For before being shipped off to Devil's Island, Dreyfus had been granted an interview with Boisdeffre, who heard him out, and assured Dreyfus that he, Boisdeffre, would now do what was needed to reverse what was plainly an unfortunate judicial error. That assurance had been what had sustained Dreyfus during his ordeal on Devil's Island, and then, at the second trial, in Rennes, he discovered that Boisdeffre had in fact been the architect of the criminal conspiracy that was the principal source of Dreyfus's ordeal. And it was that discovery, according to his grandson, that Dreyfus never quite got over. And then I remembered that such was precisely the episode, which Dreyfus never got over, that had reduced me to tears and forced me to set the translation aside. It was a consolation of sorts to realize that I felt overwhelmed precisely at that point in his story where he did, but what I want to insist on is the role that the Captain played at precisely that moment. In that episode, Dreyfus was cast as a world-class *schlemiel*, a figure who placed all his trust in his own worst enemy.

All of which leads me to wonder what special grand-filial light might be cast by Mendel Beilis' grandson during my second visit to Cardozo. If I can anticipate, I would say, on the basis of *Blood Libel*, that the idiosyncratic case of Beilis, so often cast in the role of a Russian Dreyfus, was significantly different.[2] For he was not, like Dreyfus, the man who had so disastrously misplaced his trust in his adversary, what I have called a world-class *schlemiel*. No, Beilis was

---

1 *The Affair: The Case of Alfred Dreyfus*, trans. J. Mehlman (New York: George Braziller, 1986).
2 Mendel Beilis, *Blood Libel: The Life and Memory of Mendel Beilis*, ed. by Jay Beilis, Jeremy Garber, and Mark Stein (Chicago: Beilis Publishing, 2011).

the man whose enduring and idiosyncratic sadness was that he was never given the money he thought he deserved from his fellow Jews as compensation for his suffering. The curious curse of his life, to recall Hannah Arendt's distinction, quoted in our epigraph, was to have been a world-class *schnorrer*.[3] And ultimately the claim against Bernard Malamud, whether justified or not, is a kind of exacerbation of the *schnorrer's* angry complaint. Not only was he not given what he deserved, but he was robbed of the quintessential little—the story of his life—that he had.

Now before fleshing out the profound *difference* between these two victims of anti-Semitism, let us review the extent to which Beilis and Dreyfus have been seen as versions of each other. Curiously, the identification or assimilation of the two can be found in both the Beilis memoir and the Malamud novel. At the Beilis trial, the prosecutor tells the court that "the world is in an uproar… Do you remember the Dreyfus case in France? The whole world was set agog, and why? Because he was a Jew." (155)[4] After he is freed, during a trip to Jerusalem, he is told by an Arab leader that he is one of the "three great Jewish heroes and martyrs." "One of the others he mentioned was Dreyfus" (199). The critic Alfred Kazin was apparently even prepared to make Beilis out to be an unsympathetic character simply for the sake of making him comparable to Dreyfus.

And for all the differences between Malamud's Yakov Bok (in *The Fixer*) and Mendel Beilis in his memoir, the Dreyfus reference remained a constant. Toward the end of the novel, the fixer's father-in-law tells him pointedly: "If you feel bad, think of Dreyfus. He went through the same thing with the script in French" (306).[5] And Malamud, in an interview, claimed to have added a dash of Dreyfus (and also of Vanzetti) to the ordeal of Beilis in order to render it more philosophical (as an Aristotelian might have put it) (279).

But perhaps a more refined articulation of the two sequences—Dreyfus and Beilis—is in order. And such is in fact what I had in mind when composing the title of these remarks: Dreyfus/Beilis/History/Literature. For the case might be made that both the Dreyfus Affair and the Beilis Affair

---

3 Hannah Arendt, "The Jew as Pariah: A Hidden Tradition," in Arendt, *The Jewish Writings* (New York: Knopf, 2009) p. 285.
4 Page references in the text are to *Blood Libel*, op. cit.
5 Page references to *The Fixer* in the text are to the Farrar, Straus & Giroux edition (New York, 1966).

survive culturally in a bipartite form that is alternately historical and literary. I am suggesting that the Dreyfus Affair might at some level be viewed as both the historical sequence in which Emile Zola rightly or wrongly starred *and* (at the same time) as the half-forgotten novel, titled *Vérité*, which he wrote about it.[6] And the Beilis Affair survives in culture both as the historical sequence of Mendel Beilis' ordeal and the novel which Bernard Malamud rightly or wrongly derived (or plagiarized) from it. The wager would be to gauge just what the gain (or loss) might be in envisaging or forging a domain that would seamlessly integrate history and literature.

Take the apparent disparity between the Dreyfus Affair, which turned on an alleged act of treason or military malfeasance, and the Beilis Affair, which is centered on the crime of the rape and murder of a boy—of which Beilis is wrongfully accused. Now in between the two Affairs, it happens that Zola transposed the events of the Dreyfus sequence into the story of the wrongful accusation brought against a Jewish school teacher (named Simon) for the rape and murder of a schoolboy (named Zéphirin). It is as though the Dreyfus history had to be transmuted into a fiction or dream of rape (and murder) before it could advance metonymically in time or repeat itself metaphorically in the spatiality of what Malamud calls "Russian script."

It is this quadripartite structure—a historical sequence and its transposition into a novel (by Zola) transposed into a subsequent historical sequence as it is itself transposed into a novel (by Malamud)—that interests me. To take a relatively minor case, it may be objected that the rape and murder of the child in Zola's *Vérité* has little to do with the blood libel (so central to the Beilis case), but the answer to that is found in Malamud's *Fixer*, where the accusation of ritual murder abruptly disappears from the act of indictment, and only a charge of sexual violence (and murder) appears to remain. "What had happened to the charge of ritual murder? Holding each sheet up for better light, [Bok] searched in vain. There was no such charge. Every reference to a religious crime, though hinted at, led up to, had in the end been omitted" (281). It is as though Malamud's celebrated novel of the Beilis Affair had been straining to coincide with Zola's forgotten novel of the Dreyfus Affair.

---

6 See my essay, "Zola's Novel of the Dreyfus Affair: Between *Mystique* and *Politique*" in *Jews, Catholics, and the Burden of History: Studies in Contemporary Jewry*, ed. Eli Lederhendler (Oxford: Oxford University Press, 2005).

At the same time, the superimposition of elements in our four-part structure—whose parts, we should recall, are Dreyfus, *Vérité*, Beilis, and *Fixer*—allows us to perceive what is perhaps the central or pivotal difference between the two cases. This has to do with the question of pardon or amnesty. At a key point in *The Fixer*, a former jurist comes to announce to the fixer, Malamud's surrogate for Beilis, still awaiting a trial we will never witness in the novel, that because it is the three hundredth anniversary of the rule of the house of Romanov, the Czar, despite his anti-Semitism, has decided to issue a decree of amnesty for certain classes of criminals that will include the fixer, Yakov Bok, himself. The fixer replies that he wants a "fair trial, not a pardon" (294).

The heroic logic of his reply is clear. To accept a pardon was to acknowledge guilt, and to acknowledge guilt on a charge of Jewish ritual murder was to furnish a pretext for all sorts of mass violence against the Jews in the form of pogroms. The point is crucial. For what is most interesting in the Beilis saga, I believe, is not the absurd accusation nor the immense suffering, but the decision to reject a pardon, which would have entailed an admission of guilt, and to endure the resultant suffering, in order to forestall an impending pogrom—or series of pogroms. This is the basis on which Beilis appears to have based his certainty that international Jewry, prepared to call him a martyr, owed him a fortune for his suffering, and is also the basis on which he cuts so striking a figure of what I have called a world-class *schnorrer* (or beggar) when that fortune turned out not to be forthcoming.

Significantly, this episode, which I have reported from Malamud's novel, in fact originally appears in Beilis' memoir. He is told that the Romanov dynasty is preparing to celebrate its jubilee with a manifesto pardoning all convicts at hard labor. Beilis replies: "I need no manifesto, I need a fair trial." The official then tells him that if he is ordered to be released (a decision that may have been dictated by the collapsing case against him), he would have to go. Beilis' response: "No—even if you open the doors of the prison, and threaten me with shooting, I shall not leave" (64).

Now it is precisely here that the French Dreyfus may be seen to differ from the Russian one. For Dreyfus himself, after the second verdict, at Rennes, against him, in very short order accepted the offer of pardon tendered by President Waldeck-Rousseau. And this compromise, with its implicit acceptance of guilt, has long been perceived, at least by Dreyfusard purists, as a blemish on his character. Consider Anatole France's classic summary of the Dreyfusard dilemma (or conundrum): "We would have given our lives for Dreyfus. He [Dreyfus] was not prepared to." Thus whereas Beilis was the man who rejected a pardon, and ended up living in relative poverty, Dreyfus, whose family was, of course, wealthy, accepted, after years of suffering on Devil's Island, his pardon and was almost immediately thereafter able to resume a life of relative comfort.

And if Beilis, in rejecting an offer of pardon, could reasonably lay claim to having saved his fellow Jews from extraordinary damage, Dreyfus, one is tempted to say, in accepting a pardon, did extraordinary damage to *his* co-religionists, although in this case the religion was not that of Judaism, but of French republicanism, the faith or mystique whose temples, it has been said, were the public schools, and whose decline into what Péguy called *politique* has proceeded apace ever since.

The recasting and repetition of Beilis' refusal to accept amnesty—from Beilis' memoir to Malamud's novel—is, of course, a key motif in the accusation of plagiarism in *Blood Libel*. This is no doubt because the episode, which is a moral high point of the novel, has erroneously been assumed to be an invention of the novelist. Alan Friedman calls it the novel's "supreme affirmation" (275).

We have come, then, by way of our quadri-partite structure to the question that dominates (and perhaps deserves to dominate) a discussion of the status of the Beilis Affair, the issue of what has been called Malamud's plagiarism of Mendel Beilis' memoir. I have suggested above that the odor of plagiarism exuded by Malamud's book is of a piece with the long and idiosyncratic developments in the memoir dealing with Beilis, the *schnorrer's* sense of being stripped of what is his rightful due, what had been promised him as compensation for the suffering he endured on behalf of the Jewish people. In this case, he endures his ultimate insult, when his words are, as it were, stolen out of his mouth by Malamud's alleged plagiarism—the copying of Beilis at his most sublime (i.e., his refusal of a pardon).

But the motif of copied words depriving one of one's speech turns out to be a key feature of the forgotten Zola novel, *Vérité*, which is the second panel in our quadripartite interpretative construct. For a crucial bit of evidence, the gag used to silence the child during his rape and murder, is a writing sampler, crumpled up, but belonging to the actual culprit, a wild-eyed ecclesiastic school teacher, in Zola's novelistic transcription of the Affair. That culprit, the novel's version of Esterhazy, is named Brother Gorgias, and he is the most literarily gripping character in an otherwise sentimental and minimally interesting plot.

The combination of copying (the writing sampler) and reducing to silence (the gag) in *Vérité* thus seems to gesture, in displaced manner, toward the subsequent panels in our configuration, and specifically to the situation of the Beilis memoir, plagiarized (according to *Blood Libel*) and, until recently, out of print, in part because of the threat it might pose to the success of Malamud's Pulitzer-Prize winning novel (again according to *Blood Libel*).

But it also harkens back to the very inception of the Affair (i.e., to the very first panel in our configuration). Because the writing sampler (or *modèle d'écriture*) in the mouth, the principal piece of evidence in Zola's novelistic transposition of the Affair, was inspired by the expert testimony of Alphonse Bertillon at the first Dreyfus court martial. Working for the prosecution, he claimed that the incriminating document in the Affair, the much scrutinized *bordereau* or memorandum of military secrets to be delivered to the German military attaché in Paris, had, in fact, been copied or traced by Dreyfus himself from his own "writing model," a template or *gabarit* placed beneath the relatively transparent sheet on which the incriminating letter was written. Why should he do this? According to the ingenious Bertillon, Dreyfus had traced his message so that he would be able to claim that it had been forged in the event that he had been caught with the letter on his person.

In sum, at the beginning of our four-paneled progression, we find what is alleged to be a crucial copying of a text, the *bordereau*, which in turn launches the Dreyfus Affair. At the end of our progression, we find a novel of the Beilis Affair alleged to be a crucial copying of a text, the Beilis memoir. In between the first and second panel, the Affair and Zola's novelized version of it, military corruption and treason are replaced by ecclesiastical corruption and the murder of a boy. And the second two panels are eventually characterized in Malamud's novel, as a rescripting in Russian of what was originally a French script: Beilis as the Russian Dreyfus.

Such an equivalence of our two victims, Dreyfus and Beilis, is, as we have suggested, a severe misperception of all that distinguishes Dreyfus, the world-class *schlemiel*, from Beilis, the world-class *schnorrer*. Nor does it take into account all that separates the zenith of Beilis' ordeal, his refusal of amnesty, from the nadir of Dreyfus's ordeal, his acceptance of a pardon.

And yet the almost quilted texture of our elaboration—joining historical sequence (Dreyfus) to literary transposition, and then second historical sequence (Beilis), falsely assumed to repeat the first, but joined to its own questionable literary transposition, *The Fixer*—has the merit of conveying something of the dreamscape of European anti-Semitism in all of its hybridity, and that alone, I would claim, makes it worth our consideration.

5

Paul Valéry:
Poetry and the Shape of a Life

Somewhere late in *La Recherche du temps perdu*, Proust suggests that his book is such that to read more deeply into it would inevitably be for the reader to delve more deeply into him or herself. The experience of having recently written a memoir that is in many ways an analysis of my life as a (reading) writer has led me to suspect that the reading I am most interested in is, for better or worse, such as might be amenable to the Proustian paradigm.[1] This has led me back to the writings of the man whom T.S. Eliot regarded as *the* representative European poet of the first half of the twentieth century, Paul Valéry (1871-1945), a writer I have attended to in various contexts over a number of years (1195).[2] The aim might ultimately be to "construct" a Valéry, generating a structure such that it might simultaneously serve as a medium of self-analysis, in much the spirit in which Valéry aspired to "construct" a Leonardo, or a Goethe, or even a von Moltke at different times in his life.

The danger, of course, would be to conduct that self-analysis, which would inevitably be oblique, at times unwitting, and fundamentally deferred in its temporality, independently of a concern for expanding our understanding

---

1 J. Mehlman, *Adventures in the French Trade: Fragments Toward a Life* (Stanford: Stanford University Press, 2010).
2 Page references in the text, unless otherwise indicated, are to Michel Jarrety, *Paul Valéry* (Paris: Fayard, 2008).

of our putative subject, in this case one of the world's great poets. One should not, that is, forget that one of the most persistent themes of Valéry's poetry throughout his life was the myth of Narcissus and the numerous traps (or modes of self-indulgence) it holds in store for those who would attend to it. Valéry *d'abord*, then—which circumstance leads to a consideration of why the times are particularly auspicious for a reconsideration. The reasons are twofold:

1. In 2008, a 1350-page biography of the poet—by Michel Jarrety—appeared, considerably expanding the quantity of what might be called the raw data from which the aforementioned "Paul Valéry"—in all its unexpected *fruitfulness*—might be constructed.
2. During that same year, some 150 previously unpublished poems by the poet, all of them addressed to the woman half his age whom he courted during the last years of his life, were made available to the public. The volume bore the strange title *Corona et coronilla (Crown and coronet).*[3] The fact that the recipient—or pretext— of those poems, who had chosen a masculine pen name, Jean Voilier, to enhance her literary career (as both novelist and publisher) was the subject of a separate biography that same year (2008) is a further indication of the auspiciousness of the present conjuncture for elaborating a "Valéry."[4]

Yet (the memorialist in me interjects) no sooner have I laid out the empirical grounds for wanting to turn to Valéry than I find the entire subject being drawn into the orbit of a principal development of my recent memoir. That development concerns the French writer Maurice Blanchot, a cult figure of sorts, to whom I have turned differently at different stages of my life (and who coincidently enough figures quite differently as a tutelary presence in the memoir of the late philosopher Stanley Cavell, simultaneously published in the same collection at the Stanford University Press as my own).[5] I have sometimes felt my ongoing engagement with Blanchot, and however accurate or not my interpretations of his work may have been, to be a form of self-analysis of precisely the sort I referred to at the inception of these remarks. What I see now is

3 *Corona et coronilla* (Paris: Bernard de Fallois, 2008).
4 Célia Bertin, *Portrait d'une femme Romanesque: Jean Voilier* (Paris: Bernard de Fallois, 2008).
5 Stanley Cavell, *Little Did I Know: Excerpts From Memory* (Stanford: Stanford University Press, 2010).

the extent to which each of the three phases of my engagement with Blanchot appears to beckon toward the case of Valéry, leading me to raise the question of the value to be attributed to the existence (or insistence) of that tripartite structure. Allow me, then, to evoke those three phases of Blanchot and their affinity with Valéry as a way of getting deeper (but the metaphor of depth will undergo a sea-change as we proceed) into the subject.

In the early 1970s, fascinated by the newly emergent problematic of Derrida, which had not yet settled into academic respectability, but also by the proximity to deconstruction of Blanchot, about whom Derrida would eventually write a book, I attempted to find a point of articulation between the two through a consideration of Blanchot's reading of Rilke.[6] Plainly the primacy of voice in Rilke's *Sonnets* to *Orpheus*, the stunned silence to which the beasts of the Underworld were reduced by the poet's song, were at a remove from that "deconstruction" of voice, primacy, and presence that was the specific focus of Derrida's thought. Whence my pleasure in inserting between Blanchot and Derrida a short prose text by Rilke, titled "Urgeräusch" (Primal Sound) and written at about the same time (1919) as Freud was composing "The Uncanny." It was concerned with a childhood memory of the poet: a schoolteacher's construction of a primitive phonograph issues in the stunned silence of his class when they hear their "own" voices, freshly recorded by the teacher, billowing forth to them from the machine. Now the quality of that silence is precisely that of the beasts of the Underworld reduced to muteness by Orpheus' voice. But if the beasts of the sonnets are superimposable on the children in the classroom, then the primitive phonograph, a "writing" machine separating voice from itself, is superimposable on the poet's voice. But Rilke does not stop there. A second episode in his prose text evokes the fascination exercised on him by a human skull (and particularly its cranial suture) observed in a shop window near the Ecole des Beaux-Arts in Paris. Rilke's fantasy pertains to the unbelievable "primal" sound (*Urgeräusch*) that might be produced by that suture once the "floating stylus" of the primitive phonograph is displaced onto it and allowed to run its course. The deferment and displacement of the writing apparatus apparently *internal* to voice at its most primal was thus the precise deconstructive contraption allowing for an articulation of the thought of Blanchot with that of

---

6 See M. Blanchot, *L'espace littéraire* (Paris: Gallimard, 1955).

Derrida. Perhaps the elation with which my essay, first published in France, was received is best conveyed in the dedication that Derrida inscribed in the copy of *Glas*, his own self-analysis, or so it seemed at the time, which he gave me. The word *Glas* (meaning "knell" in French) on the title page was inserted by Derrida into a line from Rilke's *Sonnets to Orpheus* (II, 13) that I had commented on in my essay: *Sei ein klingendes Glas, das sich im Klang schon zerschlug* (Be a ringing glass that shattered even as it rang).

To invoke Rilke, however, is already to be engaging Valéry, who was translated into German by Rilke. Or as Rilke himself put it in a letter to Monique Saint-Hélier, "I was alone, waiting, my entire *oeuvre* was waiting. One day I read Valéry and realized that my wait was over." (496) Valéry's prose, of course, had been the focus of an important essay of Derrida, intent on demonstrating that Freud (and Nietzsche) were "diverted sources" (*sources écartées*) of his work.[7] And it would indeed be difficult to encapsulate the core of Derrida's thought better than in Valéry's formulation: "These considerations lead one to categorize the philosopher among the artists: but such an artist is not prepared to admit that he is one, and therein lies the drama, or the comedy, of Philosophy."[8] But the deconstructive virus was already there in the poetry, as we shall see shortly, and perhaps never more so than in its affinities with Rilke. Consider Valéry's short poem "Les Grenades" in this light. A metaphor is developed of sovereign Mind as a pomegranate, savoring its inner articulations (or partitions) even as—or after—the pomegranate bursts or explodes: "Cette lumineuse rupture / Fait rêver une âme que j'eus / De sa secrète architecture." Given the simple past tense (*eus*) of *avoir*, the presence of Mind to itself, figure of what Derrida called "logocentrism," would be a mirage fostered precisely by what disrupts it (the luminous "rupture" of the seeds exploding their way out of the fruit). To say as much, however, is to all but harken back to another explosion and another odd instance of the simple past (*zerschlug*)—which we find in the Rilke line cited by Derrida in his dedication. And indeed my reading of Valéry's poetry, its "tear-work" (on the model of Freud's "dreamwork," as we shall see) an instantiation of deconstruction itself, was the subject of "On Tear-Work: *l'ar de Valéry*," which was

---

7 Jacques **Derrida**, « Qual Quelle : Les Sources de **Valéry** » in **Marges** de la « Philosophie », Paris, Editions de Minuit, 1972, pp. 325-363
8 "Introduction à la méthode de Léonard de Vinci" (Paris: Gallimard, 1957), p. 121.

written during the same years as my "Orphée scripteur: Blanchot/Rilke/Derrida," the text just evoked.[9]

The Rilke/Valéry intertext spilled into English as well. James Merrill's masterly poem, "Lost in Translation" is a meditation on a lost copy of Rilke's translation of Valéry's "Palme," a poem that Merrill himself would eventually translate. In my essay "Merrill's Valéry: An Erotics of Translation," I analyze the tear-work, secreted "dram by dram," as time itself, in Merrill's translation, but also the missing Rilke translation as metaphor for the missing piece in every puzzle as evoked in "Lost in Translation.".[10]

My early readings of both Blanchot and Valéry, and whatever attractiveness they may have held, received a considerable jolt with my discovery that Blanchot, in the 1930's, long before his emergence as the philo-semitic philosopher/critic of what Lévinas called "a passivity beyond all passivity," had been a political militant and journalist of decidedly fascist leaning, in the margins of Action Française, calling for acts of terrorism against Jews and Communists. He eventually abandoned that posture shortly before the war, once he realized that fascism was the ideology of France's national enemy, whereupon he undertook to analyze literature itself as a protracted farewell to the practice of "terror" (which was Jean Paulhan's metaphor, in *Les Fleurs de Tarbes ou la Terreur dans les lettres*, for what Derrida would eventually thematize as "logocentrism"). The result of my essays delving into this second perspective (which seemed to some a serendipitous anticipation of what later became known as the de Man affair) was an understandable though regrettable cooling of my relations with Derrida.[11] The dedications alluding to Rilke (or anyone else) would in short order cease arriving. But it is the relation to Valéry that intrigues me here. Let us assume that the inherently traumatic nature of literature, what Blanchot calls *l'écriture du désastre*, is linked to a sense of disbelief at how close the author, a militant fascist ideologue until the Munich crisis (in my reading), must have sensed he

9 "On Tear-Work: *l'ar- de Valéry*" in *Yale French Studies*, 52, Yale University Press, 1975; "Orphée scripteur: Blanchot, Rilke, Derrida" in *Poétique* 20 (Paris: Seuil, 1974).
10 J. Mehlman, "Merrill's Valéry: An Erotics of Translation" in L. Venuti, *Rethinking Translation: Discourse, Subjectivity, Ideology* (New York: Routledge, 1992).
11 J. Mehlman, "Blanchot at *Combat*: Of Literature and Terror" in *Legacies: Of Anti-Semitism in France* (Minneapolis: University of Minnesota Press, 1983) and "Iphigenia 38: Deconstruction, History, and the case of *L'Arrêt de mort*" in *Genealogies of the Text* (Cambridge, Cambridge University Press, 1995), chapter 6.

had come. Not that Blanchot, to my knowledge, ever said as much. Indeed the closest he may have come to avowing that sense of disbelief is in an article of 1984 on "Les Intellectuels en question," where he expresses his own incredulity at Valéry's failure to come to terms with the moral catastrophe of his outright support for the anti-Dreyfusard cause during the notorious *fin-de-siècle* Affair.[12]

Michel Jarrety, Valéry's biographer, observes that Valéry's stance against Dreyfus was the sole militant act of his life (245). The circumstances of his commitment are familiar. After the suicide of Colonel Henry following the revelation that he had forged a key document incriminating Dreyfus, Charles Maurras gained notoriety by speaking of Henry's crime as a patriotic act of forgery. A collection was taken up to honor the memory of Henry (and protect his widow), and it was to that monument to the memory of the forger that Valéry, in 1898, made a contribution—"not without reflection," as he put it. There were reasons, of course, for Valéry's anti-Dreyfusism. As a sometime bureaucrat employed by the Ministry of War, he would not even have needed to believe Dreyfus guilty in order to see the danger to the Army wreaked by any attempt to demonstrate his innocence. Years later, in 1931, he explained his stance during the Affair by confessing that he was capable of being absolutely pitiless toward anyone inclined to speculate on his capacity for pity (246). One of the achievements of the new biography is to reveal how deeply anti-Semitic the milieu in which Valéry moved in the period immediately before (and during) the Affair was. Pierre Louÿs, the writer and friend to whom Valéry later attributed his decision to become a poet (1140), described himself bizarrely as neither Dreyfusard nor anti-Dreyfusard, but as "Esterhazyste," and "madly (*follement*) anti-Semitic" (242), i.e., a partisan of the scoundrel whose entry into the Affair was due solely to the fact that he, Esterhazy, was the actual culprit in the act of treason falsely attributed to Dreyfus. In fact, however, the spelling of "esterhazyste" by Louÿs was illuminatingly erroneous. In writing "estherazyste," Louÿs appears to have displaced the *h* of Esterhazy and moved the case of Dreyfus into the Biblical orbit of Esther and the prospect of a mass murder of the Jews with which she was confronted. Lest that interpretation of an apparent typo seem excessive, I would recall that one of Valéry's mentors, the novelist Huysmans, who played a key role in securing the poet's employment

---

12 "Les Intellectuels en question" in *Le Débat*, 29 (1984).

at the Ministry of War, had but recently published a novel, *En rade*, which he regarded as a turning point in his career and which itself turns on a haunting dream of Biblical Esther lavishing her seductive charms on a Persian potentate in a climate of imminent doom for her people. That novel, moreover, itself takes place in a decrepit provincial castle dominated by a faint odor of ether (*éther*). It is a fragrance that eventually has the protagonist musing on the pleasures of perpetuating remembrance of the dead by recycling their characteristic fragrance in (and as) perfumed soap. We have thus moved via the two first names in Valéry's list of those who determined the course of his life: "Louÿs for poetry, Huysmans for the Ministry" (1140), from "Esterhazy" to "estheraziste" to "Esther" to "éther"—i.e., from the Dreyfus Affair to a fantasy (of flesh to soap) worthy of the Holocaust at its most grisly.[13]

We have moved, that is, from Valéry as tutelary figure for deconstruction to the poet's insertion in the history of French anti-Semitism, even as we had moved, in parallel, from Blanchot's relation to Derrida (once a bridge between the two had been supplied by Rilke) to Blanchot's own insertion in the anti-Jewish fevers of France in the 1930s. It is as though I had been working, in the case of each author, with what might be, at best, construed as a virtuoso rendition of an (aestheticizing) treble part, only to discover the existence of a rich but politically sinister bass. But we have as yet spoken rather little of Valéry's poetry per se. It is for that reason that I would at this point invite the reader to sample an already published essay that would bind "treble" to "bass" in Valéry.[14] It will take us deeper into Valéry, but its title, "Craniometry and

---

13 J. Mehlman, "Huysmans: Conversion, Hysteria, and the French 'Unconscious'" in *Notebooks in Cultural Analysis*, 2 (Durham: Duke University Press, 1985).

14 The matrix is developed in J. Mehlman, "Craniometry and Criticism" in *Genealogies of the Text*," and takes us from the "first return" to poetry of the Jeune Parque's *tear* (*larme*) as figure of the poem the poet finds himself unable *not* to write to "*la mer, la mer* toujours recommencée," the deceptive *anagram* of that *larme* in the opening strophe of "Le Cimetière marin." From there to an enigmatic liquid emission—the irretrievable bit of red wine randomly squandered in the sea in "Le vin perdu"—the path is clear. But that image is borrowed from the political context of Valéry's essay "La Crise de l'esprit" and was originally borrowed from the philosopher Henri Poincaré's discussion of the second principle of thermodynamics in *La Valeur de la science*. To these may be added the seeds of the "Grenades" in the poem we have already had occasion to invoke. A key connection between Valéry's politics and his poetry (by way of his youthful apprenticeship in craniometry with Georges Vacher de Lapouge) would draw on the superimposability of the title of the poems of Valéry's "second return" (*Corona et coronilla*) and the key opposition—in "Le cimetière marin"-- between the sun at its zenith (*tête parfaite*) and the empty skulls of the cemetery (*têtes inhabitées*).

Criticism: Notes Toward a Valeryan Criss-cross," turns out also to gesture in the direction of what I called the self-analytic dimension of this effort. For it will be recalled that our initial reading of Blanchot, establishing the terms of a "translation" of Blanchot into Derrida, ended with Rilke's fascination with a skull on display and the music that might be elicited from the displacement of a "floating stylus" onto its cranial suture.

II

The twin interpretative strata—aesthetico-deconstructive and political—treble and bass, as I termed them earlier—thus seemed to function on parallel tracks in the cases of Blanchot, the medium of my self-analysis in the memoir, and Valéry. Whereupon I found myself confronted with a third interpretative possibility, which might be called the erotic. It dawned on me somewhat anomalously when a colleague, to my surprise, recommended with some urgency that I read the newly published biography of a relatively little known twentieth-century author, Dominique Aury.[15] Aury was to achieve a modicum of notoriety fairly late in her life when it was revealed that she was the author, under a pen name, of the erotic classic *L'Histoire d'O*. In addition, she had been a leading figure (and the only woman) in the inner sanctum of the prestigious Gallimard publishing house for twenty-five years. Upon consulting the biography's table of contents, I was stunned to find a chapter titled "Jeffrey Mehlman, 'Blanchot à Combat.'" The explanation? In charting Blanchot's transition from the pre-war anti-semitic journal *Combat* to a milieu with important links to the Resistance, I had identified two tutelary figures: Thierry Maulnier, who edited the fascist-prone *Combat* in 1936, and Jean Paulhan, who was a leading figure in the intellectual Resistance. As it happens, the (clandestine) author of the erotic classic had successive clandestine love affairs with Thierry Maulnier (during his years with *Combat*) and Jean Paulhan (as of the period of his Resistance engagement). And these affairs were the sequences around which David's biography was organized. Moreover, Aury's principal epistolary confidant during both affairs appears to have been none other than Maurice Blanchot, who had

---

15 Angie David, *Dominique Aury* (Paris: Editions Léo Scheer, 2006).

fallen under her spell. In brief, my ethico-political essay on Blanchot, the subject of a polemic in France in 1983, had turned out to offer, unwittingly, a canvas of sorts for David's biography of Aury. Unless, of course, it meant that my ethico-political reading of a major transition in Blanchot's life might be better read as the record (or reflection) of a sentimental—or even lovelorn—friendship.

But once again, as with Blanchot, so with Valéry... In 2008, there appeared an anthology of 150 previously unpublished poems addressed to the love of the last seven years of Valéry's life, Jeanne Loviton, who wrote and published, as already mentioned, under the (male) pen name Jean Voilier. The collection was curiously titled (by Valéry himself) *Corona et coronilla* ("crown" and "coronet"), each of whose *gems*—and the French *gemme* is a homophone of *j'aime*, an expression of desire—would be a different poem. But no sooner have we noted the title than we may observe that with its differently sized heads, it reads like an annotation out of craniometry itself. Moreover, when Valéry first met de Gaulle at the end of the War, he noted in his *Cahiers*: "Nose quite strong, brown-haired dolichocephalic (*dolichocéphale châtain*)..." (1166) It is a term that comes out of Vacher de Lapouge. Might the notorious craniometer have left a deeper imprint on Valéry than his recent biographer appears prepared to admit?

Nowhere was Valéry's last love more agonizingly intense than in its ending. On Easter Sunday, April 15, 1945, Jean Voilier, scarcely more than half the poet's age, announced to him that she had decided to marry the publisher Robert Denoël. Valéry summoned words suitable to the occasion: "You are aware that *you alone stood between me and death*, alas, it appears that *I alone stood between you and life*." (1190) Having received her announcement like an "axe blow (*un coup de hache*)," Valéry died soon after (July 20, 1945). In newly liberated Paris, a state funeral was ordered by Charles de Gaulle.

The last months of Valéry's affair with Voilier appeared to mark another ending, that of literature itself. In the garden of her home in the Paris suburb of Auteuil, dominated by a willow tree that had become emblematic of their love, Voilier hosted a party, where Valéry read from (his) *Mon Faust*, which he occasionally referred to as the *Third Faust*. Here is Valéry's evocation of the event:

"I recall an afternoon in a garden. There were about forty people. Facing the flowers, a kind of play, which was worth whatever it may have been worth, was read. Whatever its value, that small group, the setting, the welcome, the impression of TOTAL LUXURY, of perfection attained by the effort of one individual, the taste of another, a refinement that was never excessive—in brief, the distinction of it all, constituted a kind of masterpiece… That jewel, which lasted a few hours, transported me back to a time of consummate civilization. There were no movies, and one was free to offer to a few the most exquisite flower of combined thought and elegance. I dreamt of a restoration of taste and that on the model of that garden party a reception might be envisaged, without any crowding, around a well-chosen work, and that conversation might become fashionable again. […] Yes, that garden party left me with a wondrous memory; but the heart flinches at the thought that all this will never be seen again. I see that beautiful garden with the sentiment elicited by a cemetery. There was a willow tree [*un saule*] whose death was a presentiment of misfortune. We watched it wilt and perish, the tree that had wafted so sweetly in front of happy windows. It was even sung, people say [*Il fut même chanté, dit-on*]. But that song itself will be destroyed [*Mais ce chant même sera détruit*]. Nothing must subsist [*Rien ne doit subsister*]."[16]

[Il me souvient d'un après-midi dans un jardin. Il y avait une quarantaine de personnes. On a lu en regard des fleurs, une sorte de pièce qui valait ce qu'elle valait. Quelle que fut la valeur de la pièce, cette petite assemblée, ce cadre, l'accueil, l'impression de LUXE TOTAL, de perfection obtenue par le travail de l'un, le goüt de l'autre, le choix, le raffinement sans faste—bref, la distinction de tout, cela faisait une manière de chef-d'oeuvre…. Ce joyau de quelques heures me transporta dans un temps de civilisation accomplie. Il n'y avait pas de cinéma, et l'on pouvait offrir à quelques-uns la fleur de pensée et l'élégance combinées la plus exquise. Je rêvais d'une restauration du goüt et que sur le modèle de cette partie de jardin on créât une mode de réception sans cohue, autour d'une oeuvre bien choisie, que l'on remît aussi la conversation à la mode. […] Oui, cette poétique garden-party m'a laissé un souvenir de merveille; mais le coeur défaille à la pensée que cela ne se reverra plus. Je vois le beau jardin

---

16 Quoted in Bertin, p. 220.

avec le sentiment que donne un cimetière. Il y eut là un saule dont la mort fut un présage de malheur. On l'a vu se flétrir, dépérir, lui qui avait flotté si doucement devant des fenêtres heureuses. Il fut même chanté, dit-on. Mais ce chant même sera détruit. Rien ne doit subsister…"]

The end of love was thus all but contemporaneous with a certain end of literature. Indeed Valéry wrote a virtual farewell to poetry in late April 1945 on a sheet of paper that survives in the Library of the University of Texas. He quotes a line from the poem on the willow tree: "Tremble, tombe légère, un souffle t'aime, SAULE" (10), then attributes intuition to the tree: "The willow tree has died [*Le SAULE est mort*]. It had figured things out. It chose not to bear witness to what might be seen through the window… And my poems, my poor poems, composed with all my art and all my heart, they too must perish…" (10). The tutelary role of the willow for both love and literature is significant to the extent that we are dealing with a tree said to "weep" or shed tears: "Songe au saule pleureur qui pleure ses pleurs d'arbre" (72). For trees are fully participant in what I have called tear-work. We have already seen, for example, Valéry's palm tree secreting "dram by dram," in Merrill's translation, its store of light. Trees are what mark for the poet a dialectical complementarity of origin and end, depth and height. In "Palme," as we have seen:

"La substance chevelue
Par les ténèbres élue
Ne peut s'arrêter jamais,
Jusqu'aux entrailles du monde,
De poursuivre l'eau profonde
Que demandent les sommets" (155)

[In Merrill's less than ideal translation:

Their shaggy systems, fed
Where shade confers with shade,
Can never cease or tire,
At the world's heart are found
Still tracking that profound
Water the heights require.]

And just as the axis of "altitude," both height and depth, height as depth, in "Le Cimetière marin," seemed both exceeded and enabled by tear-work as a mode of writing, so does the willow exist by virtue of its capacity to weep. The tear-work of the major poems resurfaces at the end by way of the weeping willow. As the poet wrote ironically of the tree (with reference to himself): "That historic tree is affecting his mind, and if I weren't a physician (i.e., a skeptic), I would counsel him to seek treatment."[17] Less ironically, he would lament, in a letter, his misplacement of a poem he called "Le Saule," then go on to speculate on a poetry that might be a "refuge" in which "beauties, tenderness, and divine values lie dormant, in expectation [*dans l'attente*], and weep in silence [*pleurent en silence*] beneath magical slumber, without knowing it."[18] The reference to tears shed unwittingly in sleep seems a sentimentalization of the circumstance at the beginning of "La Jeune Parque"—i.e., at the inception of the poetry of Valéry's maturity.[19]

If 1944-1945 marked the end of Valéry's love, and of his poetry as well, it also marked the collapse of the German occupation of France. The garden party of August 1944, beneath the dying willow tree, was one of the final literary events of the Occupation. (Paris would be liberated later that month.) There might appear to be, that is, an apocalyptically "Visconti" side to Valéry's end. It brings together the "tear-work" (in a degraded, sentimentalized mode); the craniometry (in the very title—*Corona et coronilla*—of the final collection, degraded again, in relation to the solar corona of high noon in "Le Cimetière marin"); the poetic reinvestment of the Germanic myth, *Faust, par excellence*; and the collapse of the Nazi regime. Add to the mix Valéry's wartime notation that he found himself in tears singing the theme of Hans Sachs' duet with Eva from *Die Meistersinger*, an opera whose role in France's collaboration with the Germans I have discussed elsewhere, and the notion of Valéry's end as a climax ready-made for Visconti seems attractive indeed. (1109)[20] What, after all, might be more appropriate than the spectacle of the author who began his

---

17 Bernard de Fallois, "Postface," *Corona et coronilla* (Paris: Bernard de Fallois, 2008), p. 200.
18 Ibid., p. 199.
19 The tear-work, it should be recalled, was, in my original formulation, philosophical (rather than sentimental) in its import: the system of writing, what Derrida might have called *archi-écriture*, that underwrote the major poems.
20 "Literature and Collaboration: Benoist-Méchin's Return to Proust" in *Genealogies of the Text: Literature, Psychoanalysis, and Politics in Modern France* (Cambridge: Cambridge UP, 1995).

career under the auspices of Huysmans, high priest of the Decadent movement, ending his days as a character out of Visconti?

Yet I believe such an interpretation would be wrong. The first key to the limitations of such a view of Valéry's end relates to his relative indifference to the political world around him. As he summed up his attitude to the Occupant with characteristic diffidence in 1942: "Je suis bouddhiste, je boude." [*bouder*=to sulk or pout] (1136) At the end of the war, Julien Benda noted that one of the most dithyrambic statements in praise of Pétain during his visit to Paris in 1944 had been penned by Valéry and linked it to the career of a writer who had, after all, begun his career as a militant anti-Dreyfusard.[21] And Valéry's words about the man whom he had officially welcomed to the Académie française in 1931 do indeed sound like those of a diehard Pétainiste: "But the task of expressing the sentiment of veneration and gratitude of the illustrious and immense city would require of the writer a majesty and monumentality of style hard to imagine. Marble would be the appropriate medium."[22] But there is the attenuating circumstance (if it be such) that Valéry's words were written in 1942, although read publicly in 1944, and, more seriously, the fact that he had by then already intervened to block a statement of support for Pétain issuing from the Academy (1086). The poet's most daring statement during the war may have been his eulogy in 1941, delivered at the Academy, upon the death of Henri Bergson, who had put off an envisioned conversion to Christianity out of solidarity with his fellow Jews. In Valéry's concluding words: "Bergson already seems to belong to a bygone age, and his name, the last great name of the history of European intelligence." (1097). The question then is raised of the path taken by Valéry from militant anti-Dreyfusard to principal eulogist of Bergson. And the poetry, we shall see, plays a role in providing an answer.

That answer entails the assemblage of a series of elements:

1. The fact that the poems of *Corona et coronilla* are addressed to the woman with whom Valéry was desperately in love may serve as a reminder that when Valéry, in 1892, decided to abjure poetry as deleterious to Mind, he was simultaneously recovering from an intense

---

21 "Le cas Valéry: un poète de cour" in Julien Benda, *Les Cahiers d'un clerc* (Paris: Emile-Paul, 1949), pp. 237-240.
22 "Un Ecrit de Valéry" in Alfred Fabre-Luce, *Le Mystère du maréchal* (Geneva: Editions du cheval ailé, 1945), pp. 161-161).

infatuation with a woman in Montpellier (Madame de R.) whom he was too timid to approach. Indeed the decision to abandon poetry was concomitant with a paradoxically tender renunciation of tenderness: "Je me fis l'Ennemi du Tendre," as he would later write, somewhat archaically, "de toutes les forces de ma tendresse désespérée" (117). And returning to his crisis of 1892 during the war, he would write: "I had to invent myself and dig at a depth that was not mine in order to fight against the bite (*la morsure*) of a first great love" (1104). There appears, that is, to have been a sexual component both to the decision to write poems (but "La Jeune Parque" was said to be an "involuntary" epic) and (above all) to the decision *not* to write them. The poems of Valéry's first "return" to poetry (in 1913-1917 and later in the poems of *Charmes*, 1922), but even more those of his second "return" (1938-1945) figure as returns of the repressed.

2. But what of the agent or instrument of repression, what Freud called the ego and Valéry his "Moi de Moi"? (1104). It is here that Valéry's cult of Intelligence enters the picture, which also entails his formative relation to the theorist of intelligence with whom he was associated at the time, Vacher de Lapouge. "Ma spécialité, c'est mon esprit," as he put it (152). Method and control are the buzzwords in this phase—as is indicated by the titles "La Conquête méthodique" and "Introduction à la méthode de Léonard de Vinci." An admiration for Cecil Rhodes, the "Napoleon of the Cape," as Valéry called him, surfaces as well at this point in Valéry's life (195). Curiously, Mallarmé, whose leading disciple Valéry is frequently—and not inaccurately— deemed to be, enters Valéry's thinking in this anti-poetic phase. The links are numerous. Just as Mallarmé famously pursued a vast, unpublishable project, of immense scope, which he called *Le Livre*, "explication orphique de la Terre," so Valéry, *against* his poetry, would spend hours each morning cultivating (his) Mind in his numerous *Cahiers*. Mallarmé became associated for Valéry with the *decapitation* of poetry: "I met Mallarmé *after* undergoing his extreme influence, and at the precise moment I was guillotining literature within me, [*et au moment même où je guillotinais intérieurement la littérature*]" (105). It has been observed that Valéry was born the same year as Mallarmé's cherished son Anatole,

who died in childhood. That coincidence can indeed take us further along the path of Valéry's oedipal relation to his senior. Valéry, in fact, met his wife-to-be for the first time at Mallarmé's funeral in 1898, and in his subsequent list of the friends who had influenced him in the course of his life, if Pierre Louÿs was given the portfolio Poetry, Mallarmé was assigned that of Marriage (1140). Thus the relation between Valéry and Mallarmé may be said to be oedipal ("J'ai adoré cet homme extraordinaire dans le temps même que j'y voyais la seule tête,—hors de prix!—à couper, pour décapiter toute Rome," 154), but within an understanding of psychoanalysis closer, say, to Laplanche than to Lacan: Mind or Intelligence would be to (the tear-work of) poetry much as the ego would be to the unconscious in Freud, but the oedipal would be on the side of the *binding* or structural agent of repression rather than on that of the repressed.[23]

3. As for what happened to that structure, which I have sketched in its original purity, a consideration of Valéry's (somewhat corrupting) finances are in order at this juncture. Valéry lived under the assumption that it was the obligation of those around him to help him, given his brilliance, to find a sinecure such that he might be able to pursue his intellectual interests. Note that this did not mean publishing poetry, since he would periodically insist that he was not a poet, but rather cultivating (his) Mind every morning in the form of annotations in the numerous *Cahiers* that he never published during his lifetime. In 1900, shortly after resigning from the tedium of a bureaucratic post at the Ministry of War, he appeared to have landed a dream job as private secretary of Edouard Lebey, director of an international press agency, the Agence Havas. As the aging Lebey declined ever further into decrepitude and aphasia, Valéry became something of a nursemaid for his employer, a circumstance that maintained until Lebey's death in 1922. On the date of Lebey's death, an annotation in the *Cahiers* reads: "*Mort du patron.* Here I stand, ready to be sold or rented" (510). Thereafter, Valéry, around whom a consensus was building, on the basis of "La Jeune Parque," that he might be France's premier poet,

---

23 For Laplanche's critique of Freud's notion of "castration" as the "bedrock" of the repressed, see his *Problématiques II: Castration, symbolisations* (Paris: P.U.F, 1961).

but who wrote relatively few poems, and who was even apt, in keeping with his oath of 1892, to say that he wasn't even a poet, discovered the cash value of de luxe re-editions. As Georges Duhamel put it in 1937: "No other poet, in a very long time, will have practiced the art of turning poetry into cash to this extent" (1009). Or as the poet himself was said to have told his son François, urging him to greater diligence in his studies: "You should be aware that *La Jeune Parque* will not be able to be transformed into *rôti de veau* indefinitely" (547).

France's "greatest poet," meanwhile, had become a value in the world of French salons, the prize catch of many an ambitious hostess. In 1923, the "Amis de Paul Valéry" was founded on the principle that subscribers would pay copious dues in exchange for first editions of works by Valéry, whose cash value was indeed beginning to climb. Natalie Barney, who translated Valéry for publication in *The Dial*, eventually objected that "the paper used in such arrangements was beginning to gain in value what the text was losing…" (701)

If poetry, in the poetry vs. mind opposition that structured Valéry's mental universe, was turning into the increasingly profitable commerce of de luxe editions, mind (or intelligence) was turning into a host of official honors, but also into a plethora of invitations to lecture on a variety of subjects on which a propagandist for universal intelligence could not very well plead incompetence. The lectures turned him into an official orator—indeed, some said, the Bossuet—of the Third Republic. The honors consisted of election to the Académie française and the Collège de France, appointment as administrator of the new Centre universitaire méditerranéen in Nice and as head of the Commission on Arts and Letters of the League of Nations. To the extent that such service came with a stipend, Valéry was vulnerable to accusations of greed, none more stinging than Léon Daudet's reference to him in 1936 as "le grand prébendier," an expert in remunerations (955).

The attack by Daudet, leading member of Action Française and editor of its newspaper, is particularly significant since Daudet had been a close friend of Valéry's and a key player in arranging the publication of *L'Introduction à la méthode de Léonard de Vinci*. Somewhere along the line, Valéry, a man of the right, had invested the affect that he had previously lavished on the French nation onto the continent of Europe. To do so in the interwar years was to be pleading the common interests of all Europeans and thus the cause of peace.

This was something with which the fiercely anti-German members of Action française could have no truck. Whence the opposition to Valéry. But to argue the interests of *Homo europaeus*, we have seen, was to revert to a word dear to Vacher de Lapouge in his book *L'Aryen*. Valéry, we know, was capable of waxing lyrical on the subject of Pétain. Indeed, in a letter to an anti-Semitic friend early in the war he could even envisage, if not quite endorse, an "elimination" of the Jews (1081). But the pressures of the international society whose darling he had become had (fortunately) corrupted the original passions of Valéry's structure. And the cult of intelligence had brought him into contact too close with a number of Jews (Bergson and Einstein in particular) for him to be able to sustain the original exclusionary passions that may have motivated the anti-Dreyfusard he had been. The corruption of the structure, however, also had the result of undoing the essential opposition—between poetry and intelligence—on which Valéry had constructed his existence. He was soon viewed as the "intellectualist" poet par excellence.[24] Valéry's second return to poetry, this time as the vehicle of a devastating passion, seems like a return of the repressed intent on smashing the middling synthesis that Valéry, for whom the cash he could get for both his poems (as republished) and his lectures (as tokens of Intelligence itself) had served as a kind of solvent. That return of the repressed—poetry as passion at its most threatening—may be the ultimate import of the poems of *Corona et coronilla*.

---

24 See Jarrety's reference to this mischaracterization : "la figure si fameuse et si fausse du poète de l'intellect" (118).

6

Interpreting [with] Laplanche

On the occasion of the recent publication in English of the volume titled *Dictionary of Untranslatables,*[1] a translation of Barbara Cassin's massive *Vocabulaire européen des philosophies: Dictionnaire des intraduisibles*[2] and a volume saluted in a recent issue of the *New Yorker* by Adam Gopnik as perhaps "the weirdest book the twenty-first century has so far produced,"[3] a book whose untranslatability, moreover, it happens to have befallen me, in part, to translate, it struck me as of particular interest that the very first sentence of the American edition's preface should include a telling reference to Laplanche and Pontalis' *Vocabulaire de a psychanalyse,* identified as a key juncture in the genealogy of the more recent volume.[4] For the reference to the *Vocabulaire* at the threshold of what is arguably the century's "weirdest" book is a reminder of just how strange an accomplishment in the history of reading the Laplanche and Pontalis volume remains. And of how much it has in common with the more recent project. For like the *Dictionary of Untranslatables,* the *Vocabulaire* was, in a word, a multilingual effort, rooted in a sense that French might provide the

1 *Dictionary of Untranslatables: A Philosophical Lexicon* (Princeton: Princeton University Press, 2014).
2 *Vocabulaire européen des philosophies: Dictionnaire des intraduisibles* (Paris: Seuil and Dictionnaires Robert, 2004).
3 Adam Gopnik, "Word Magic" in *The New Yorker,* May 26, 2014, p. 36.
4 *Vocabulaire de la psychanalyse* (Paris: P.U.F., 1967). Translated by D. Nicholson-Smith, *The Language of Psychoanalysis* (New York: Norton, 1974).

wherewithal to pry open the distance separating (Freud's) German from itself. And that is the case even as English, and above all American English, would appear (or at least in 1967 *did* appear) to be mobilized in resistance to that very attempt at prying open the German.[5]

Now one reason we know all this is that Laplanche himself undertook to cull the most important lessons to be gleaned from the *Vocabulaire* in a separate volume titled *Life and Death in Psychoanalysis*.[6] Here, in a word, is how that reading worked. For each of an extensive series of key terms in Freud, Laplanche succeeded in demonstrating that there were two apparently incompatible concepts at work. Moreover, if one were to string together the first of those meanings for each doubly inscribed term, one would arrive at one interpretative scheme, which we may call Scheme A. And if one were to string together the second meaning for each of those terms one would arrive at a second interpretative scheme, which we may call Scheme B. We are thus left with two interpretative schemes (A and B) battling it out to invest a single terminological apparatus, a situation which is quite intriguing. But this is only the beginning. For the truly interesting phase of Laplanche's reading, which he never made as explicit as he might have, is that whereas one scheme, say: B, seemed to exist in total ignorance or innocence of the other (scheme A), what A turned out to mediate was nothing so much as a theory of the inevitability of the error constituted by the second scheme (B). Put in other terms: if Freud's ultimate subject were a certain irreducibility of repression, then his theory of repression itself would be subject to being repressed—whence the inevitability of the error *about psychoanalysis or repression itself* constituted by what we have called Scheme B, a different interpretation of the very same words that had been used to elaborate the theory of repression in the first place. Such was the Laplanchian lesson, I believe, to be derived from a systematic reading of the *Vocabulaire de la psychanalyse*: psychoanalysis as a kind of self-consuming artifact. And the structure of that reading was that of a criss-cross or chiasmus.

---

5 The entire sequence is not without resembling a parody of de Gaulle's reading of World War II: it would have befallen the French to split the German citadel in two were it not for the Anglo-American pact to make sure that such a defeat (of the Germans by the French) not take place.
6 *Vie et mort en psychanalyse* (Paris: Flammarion, 1970). English translation by J. Mehlman, *Life and Death in Psychoanalysis* (Baltimore: Johns Hopkins University Press, 1976).

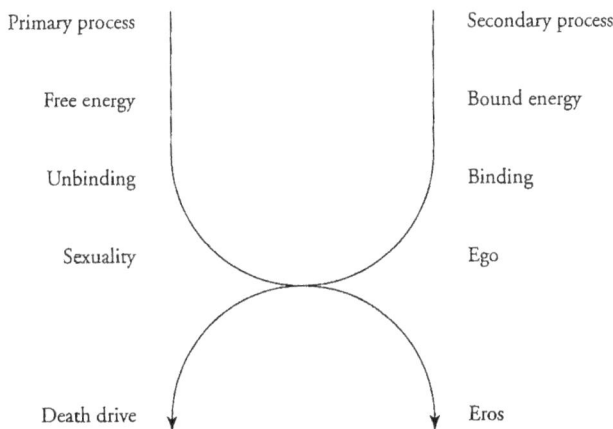

FIGURE I. The hidden structure of Freud's metapsychology. From Jean Laplanche, *Life and Death in Psychoanalysis* (Baltimore: Johns Hopkins University Press, 1976), p. 124.

At a certain point, the "pleasure principle," the soul of libidinal circulation in the unconscious, becomes the name of the nourishing principle of Eros, as it builds larger and larger libidinal units, i.e., as it ultimately comes to figure the narcissistically constituted ego, which is on the side of repression rather than on that of what is repressed…

In summary, then: the unconscious is a structure that plays havoc with every deliberate speech act, and the shape of that structure is a chiasmus.

And then, as Laplanche began to consolidate his theory, it seemed to some of us who saw in *Life and Death in Psychoanalysis* a touchstone or *nec plus ultra* of readerly complexity, the model changed. Consider the following. One of the more exquisite moments in Laplanche's reading of Freud coincided with the implicit realization that the movement whereby the drive, *propped* on the instinct, attained an autonomy of its own, was inseparable from a residual form of "seduction" whereby, say, the maternal unconscious succeeded in virtually "seducing" or displacing or peeling off the drive, become a kind of "new foundation" for whatever might be at stake in psychoanalysis, from the instinct. The genesis from within of the drive, "propped" on the instinct, would be ultimately inseparable from the genesis from without via seduction, and that no matter how complicated the temporality of the process.[7]

And then, in a book called *Nouveaux fondements pour la psychanalyse*, everything changed.[8] The "new foundation" was to be the seduction theory itself and it would assume its new importance at the expense of the very "propping" of what was after all the "new foundation" of the drive. The very term "new foundation" in Laplanche seemed to participate in a logic of double inscription of the sort that Laplanche had tracked down in Freud. The result was less the shimmering, differential beauty of what has always seemed to me one of the great acts of reading of the twentieth century than a will to assert the fundamental anthropological truth of the human condition, which is that a variety of seduction, the basis of the unconscious, was the ontological ground of our humanity.

And what was seduction as newly construed by Laplanche? Not a sexual assault of the sort that Freud famously abandoned as a hypothesis in his letter of September 1897 to Fliess, but nothing that might be considered as essentially structural either. No, the "new foundation," the very core of the unconscious, was to be a speech act of sorts, contaminated by unconscious sexuality on the adult's part and which the child or infant would spend a lifetime misinterpreting over and again in an attempt to figure out what the aim of that speech act might have been. Think of it rather as the *"confuses paroles"* emitted by the *"vivants piliers,"* the strangely insensitive parents, stony in their impassiveness, of Baudelaire's poem, "Correspondances." Or rather: the unconscious per se would be the failures or residues of such acts of interpretation or translation (of those "confuses paroles"), precisely what resists translation, which, it will be recalled, was Robert Frost's definition of poetry.

Above all, the unconscious, in Laplanche's new dispensation (and to the extent that it was the precipitate of a perverse speech act of sorts), was not to be understood in terms of structure. In Laplanche's terms: "Has there ever been

---

7 My translation of *Anlehnung* as "propping" was never fully accepted by Laplanche, who would have preferred "leaning-on." On the other hand, "propping," I am told, was received by the critic Harold Bloom as a master stroke because of its resonance with Wordsworth's characterization of the maternal breasts in *The Prelude* as "the props of my affections."

8 *Nouveaux fondements pour la psychanalyse* (Paris: P.U.F., 1987). English translation by David Macey, *New Foundations for Psychoanalysis* (London: Blackwell. 1989).

anything less sexual than the tragedy of Sophocles?"[9] The Oedipus complex, to the extent that its function was structural, was on the side of repression and not, as the Lacanians (but also Freud) would have it, on the side of the repressed.

In sum, in the fullness of its evolution, Laplanche's work assumed the shape of a chiasmus as much as Freud's did (in Laplanche's reading): an original configuration which saw a structural unconscious playing havoc with every speech act, the province of the ego, gave way to an unconscious elicited by a speech act and which might only be (further) repressed by anything smacking of the structural, said to be the province of the ego.

Consider now an exemplary case of the genesis of the unconscious as it surfaces in the first chapter of Laplanche's *Entre séduction et inspiration: l'homme*, which dates from 1999.[10] It takes us from seduction (in the familiar sense) to revelation (of a religious sort) by way of persecution (as exemplified by what Laplanche regarded as Freud's most gripping text on religion, the analysis of the Schreber case). Throughout, Laplanche's focus is to shore up the claims for a kind of primal address emanating from the other and quite distinct from any projection of fantasy allowing one to pull the rabbit of otherness out of the hat of selfhood.

Now on the subject of religious revelation, Laplanche is quite idiosyncratic. He calls on the German idealist philosopher Fichte, patron saint of German nationalism at its most fanatical, but precisely from a period in his career that preceded his "delusional" idealism, an idealism no less delusional, we are told, than that period of Freud's thought in which he too was intent on generating an outside solely on the basis of an imagined interiority (pp. 18-19). For before the delusional idealism, Laplanche tells us, Fichte had published an idiosyncratic text on religion titled *Attempt at a Critique of All Revelation*.[11] And it is this pre-idealist text of Fichte that corresponds in Laplanche's mind to the period of Freud's thought when the seduction hypothesis, in however crude a manner, was still alive as an option for Freud.

Specifically, what exercises Fichte is the dimension of address in which every act of revelation seems rooted. Revelation is inseparable from the enigma

---

9 "Mythes et théorie" in *Entre seduction et inspiration: l'homme* (Paris: P.U.F.), p. 290.

10 "Séduction, persécution, révélation " in *Entre séduction et inspiration: l'homme* (Paris: P.U.F., 1987).

11 Translated by G. Green (Cambridge: Cambridge University Press, 2010).

of whatever the revealer *intends* by what it is that he reveals. Laplanche is much taken with this and particularly with the German term used by Fichte: *Bekanntmachung* or "making known." Now no sooner does Laplanche attend to this word than he seems to relinquish the possibility of translating it, telling us that "*Bekanntmachung*," during the German occupation, was the heading found on notices plastered on walls, which, out of derision, or perhaps through an influence of surrealism, "we" had deformed into "*bécane machin*" (p. 36). Such is an example in a nominally theoretical text on the unconscious of what Laplanche calls the "refuse (*déchet*) of translation." (p. 258) Now that phrase in French has been translated by Philip Slotkin in Britain as the "thingummy contraption" (184), which, of course, nicely captures the "anything goes," "n'importe quoi," or "floating signifier" aspect of the unconscious. (Years earlier, I had reached the conclusion that what was uncanny about the Freudian uncanny was that absolutely anything might become uncanny.)[12]

At the same time, how bizarre that the Nazi occupation (*Bekanntmachung*) should provide a model, however twisted, of the unconscious… More curious still when one realizes that Laplanche offers in a footnote in the same text as an example of seduction per se, executed indirectly by German soldiers in the only French available to them, the words: "*Promenade, mademoiselle?*" (14) So: of the three categories investigated in his text—seduction, persecution, and revelation—both revelation (*Bekanntmachung*) and seduction ("Promenade, mademoiselle?) brought him and me, his reader, back to World War II and the German occupation. Not so for persecution, which was illustrated by a speculative reading of the Schreber case—without apparent reference to the war.[13] But then the connection between persecution and the occupation was so direct as to make it, one might assume, only minimally available to investment by the unconscious. And then, I was taken aback by an echo provoked in me, but perhaps in Laplanche as well, by the very model of the enigmatic message as he conceived it. The focus is a kind of exclusion of the recipient: "Je te montre…quelque chose que, par définition, tu ne peux comprendre…"

---

12 See J. Mehlman, "*Poe pourri*: Lacan's Seminar on 'The Purloined Letter'" in *Aesthetics Today*, ed. M. Philipson and P. Gudel, (New York: Meridian, 1980), p. 425.
13 The link between religious revelation and persecution, however, is tellingly discussed in comments on the persecution of Job and the enigma it constituted, *Entre seduction et inspiration: l'homme*, p.48.

(p. 14) The words were a virtual transcription of a sentence once addressed to me in a restaurant in the Place des Vosges by Jacques Lacan: "Je vais vous dire quelque chose que vous n'allez pas comprendre…" My question had been about his opinion of the recently published *Anti-Oedipe*. His answer was that I would have to read him (Lacan) on Dr. Schreber, the very figure who would be the focus of Laplanche's development on "persecution" in the text under consideration.

If there were such a thing as a "convergence of unconsciouses" (Laplanche's?, my own?), I seemed to be heading there.

Let us return to the *Bekanntmachung* (let it be known) or *bécane machin* "thingummy contraption," culled from Fichte, in a text originally published by Fichte anonymously in 1792 and widely attributed to Kant, Fichte having, so to speak, *be-Kanted* himself. It happens that I have recently been engaged in retranslating the volume in which the *Bekanntmachung* comments of Laplanche appear and wanted to come up with something more acceptable to American ears than the "thingummy contraption" of British provenance. In so doing, I discovered that the primary meaning of *bécane* in French is in fact a "machine." For better or worse, I came up with "whatchamacallit" for *machin* and thus for the entire phrase the "whatchamacallit machine." This meant, of course, that the lexical match was not between "machine" and *machin*, but chiastically, between "machine" and "*bécane*."

Now I remain enough of a Laplanchian to want to say that this was what he, in *Life and Death*, would call a "call to order," to chiastic order, coming from the unconscious. It will be recalled that chiasmus was the figure structuring the metapsychology of Freud in *Life and Death*, but also the figure structuring the relation between speech act and structure in the transition from *Life and Death* to *New Foundations*. So the chiastic switch or swerve from English "machine" away from French "*machin*" was, as it were, a call back to chiasmus and the beauties of *Life and Death*, a book that had transfixed me.

But I sensed there was something deeper. About thirty years ago, in a text I called "Writing and Deference: The Politics of Literary Adulation," a title for which Derrida never forgave me, I found myself attending to a series of texts by Jean Paulhan and particularly to a series of speculations related to what he called a linguistic "principle of counteridentity," centered on the role played by homophonic antonyms.[14] The example that most intrigued me involved the reversal at the core of the apparent transcription of German *Sauerkraut* into French *choucroute*. For what most intrigued Paulhan was that despite appearances, *croute* did not translate *Kraut* but its chiastic other, *chou* (cabbage).

Switch now to Laplanche (as he is about to reappear in English) and the case of *Bekanntmachung* or *bécane machin*. What is most interesting in English "whatchamacallit machine" is that English "machine," despite appearances, does not translate *machin*, but its chiastic other, "*bécane*."

But things can be taken further. In *De la paille et du grain*, the text of 1947 in which Paulhan offered his excursus on linguistic "counteridentity," he presented a political coefficient to the very structure of counteridentity we have been discussing. In a word, Paulhan, who was a hero of the Resistance, claimed after the war that there was no basis for the Comité national des écrivains (CNE), organ of the Resistance, to claim the moral high ground since its members, before the war, had nursed dreams of collaborating…with Moscow. Even as the wartime collaborationists had been preparing their French-patriotic resistance to just such a collaboration before the war. Such would be the chiastic principle of counteridentity as it worked its way through French politics before, during, and after the war, and such would be the basis of the amnesty for acts of collaboration and resistance that Paulhan, himself a hero in the Resistance, would call for. *Résistants* with the souls of collaborators; collaborators with the souls of *résistants*. *Bonnet blanc et blanc bonnet*, as Paulhan put it in 1947 in a political context. Or: *Sauerkraut and choucroute* in a linguistic one. To which we may add, thanks to Laplanche, *Bekanntmachung* /"*bécane machin*" in a psychoanalytic context that is not without political reverberations.[15]

But by now the reader will have realized the extent to which questions of translation, which Laplanche placed at the heart of psychoanalysis, have led

---

14 See J. Mehlman, "Writing and Deference: The Politics of Literary Adulation" in *Genealogies of the Text: Literature, Psychoanalysis, and Politics in Modern France* (Cambridge: Cambridge University Press, 1995), p. 105.

15 "*Bécane machin*," the reverse repetition of *Bekanntmachung*, is a phrase used to refer to a second-hand bicycle. I have the distinct recollection of Laplanche telling me that when in the Resistance, his task was to convey secret messages concealed in the tire or handle-bar of his bike. The relation between the call to collaboration (*Bekanntmachung*) and the act of resistance it was made to conceal (in a *bécane machin*) is a model whose pertinence would appear to be both psychoanalytical and political.

me to unconscious concerns that may be as much my own as Laplanche's. I have never been psychoanalyzed or at least I felt I had never been psychoanalyzed until my last visit with Laplanche *agonistes* at the Chateau de Pommard. He was connected to his oxygen tank and would die not long after. He had read my memoir *Adventures in the French Trade*, adding to my bemusement: "*j'y ai bien reconnu tes amours anti-sémites.*" The implication was that any subject of ongoing fascination can only be sustained by a libidinal investment. (And French anti-semitism, as a glance at my bibliography made clear, had long since become a subject of fascination for me.[16]) For better or worse I felt that afternoon that I had been analyzed by Jean Laplanche.

And if I had missed his point, it was as though he had repeated it at the end of the text on seduction, persecution, and revelation. For the principal example of the kind of address he associated with revelation (i.e., the *Bekanntmachung* and all the freight it bears with it) is the very essence of the Jewish faith and the enigmatic message at its heart: "Shema Yisrael: Hear oh Israel!"

But where does that leave us? Or rather, since psychoanalysis, if it is to have any validity, must be highly individualized, where did that leave me? The answer, at its most succinct, is that it left me in a world stretched taut between *Bekanntmachung* (or the Nazi occupation of France) and *Shema Israel* (or Judaism). It was a world of life and death, *vie et mort*, and it was the world into which, at the beginning of 1944, but displaced to the United States, I was born.

And there, via Laplanche, lay the opening of a world in which I experienced a certain revelation almost fifty years ago, bearing the name of *Vie et mort en psychanalyse*. For I have spent a considerable part of my life as a reader attempting to rediscover the kind of complexity that Laplanche had revealed in Freud, but displaced onto—or infused into--other texts.

And such would be the *transfert en creux*, the "hollowed out transference" to which Laplanche would direct me, allowing its wound to stay open in the enigma of the several words he addressed to me and which I have ever since found it difficult to transcribe without a tremor: "J'y ai bien reconnu tes amours antisémites."[17]

---

16 The most pertinent text in this context would be my *Legacies of Anti-Semitism in France* (Minneapolis: University of Minnesota Press, 1983).

17 For my own premonition of what Laplanche had intuited, see my Introduction to *Genealogies of the Text*, pp. 1-6.

7

A Biblical Genealogy of French Letters
(Lecture in Jerusalem, January 2016)

Approaching Mount Scopus, one is immediately reminded of debts one has incurred to the Hebrew University and members of its faculty. In my own case, I should say that given the role played by the writings of such towering figures as Gershom Scholem (on "redemption through sin") or Zeev Sternhell (on the "French origins of fascism"), the particular reverence that I feel for the institution should not come as a surprise. If I choose, however, to emphasize my heart-felt debt, it is because my most recent book, a memoir titled *Adventures in the French Trade*, has been particularly keen on moments of intersection between whatever my critical or intellectual achievements may have amounted to, on the one hand, and events of particular intensity in my life, on the other. These remarks have been composed, then, within that perspective or at that crossroads.

**

Of the various casualties occasioned by the attack in Paris on the satirical magazine *Charlie Hebdo* a little more than a year ago, not the least may have been the suspicion, nursed by many a professor of French literature, that if the end of his or her world—the world of the *graphosphere*, of the academic study of literature, of declining enrollments—should come, it would be, to recall a familiar line, "not with a bang but a whimper." And the grounds for that melancholy surmise, the arraying of the line out of Eliot among the casualties of the attacks in Paris, lay in the fact that on January 7, 2015, a day of spectacular violence, *Charlie hebdo* featured on its cover a caricature not of the Prophet (to be avenged) but of a novelist—specifically, the notorious winner of the Prix Goncourt of 2010, Michel Houellebecq. It was, moreover, the date of publication of his controversial novel *Soumission*. Now *Submission*, of course, is a translation of the word "Islam." So the subject of Houellebecq, who has made more than one provocative statement about Islam, could easily be filed under the rubric of "avenging the Prophet." But I would rather insist on the profoundly *written* and even literary texture of the sensibility surrounding the violence of January 7. For François, the protagonist of *Soumission*, is not only a writer but a professor of literature. What then needs be said of the relation between the January attack and literature? What follows is a set of reflections, some fortuitous, some rather personal—by a professor of French literature, myself—on the January attacks and offered, so to speak, from the depths of the graphosphere, there where writing reigns—or perhaps no longer reigns—supreme.

The novel relates in the mode of futurist or dystopian fiction a political and electoral crisis in a France in which the National Front appears to be on the cusp of becoming the majority electoral party in the country. The sole solution for the parties of the center-right and center-left turns out to consist in forming an alliance against the extreme–right wing juggernaut of Marine LePen by enlisting the complicity of a new party, the Muslim Brotherhood, relatively moderate in its religiosity, and which will emerge triumphant in the second round of voting and proceed to form a government.

But what shall we say of François, the protagonist professor of French literature? His field of expertise is the work of Huysmans, the late nineteenth century author of *A rebours*, that breviary of European "decadence" and favorite book of the Oscar Wilde hero, Dorian Grey. Now it happens that I was engaged in rereading that very novel at the time of the Paris attacks and I would like to speak of that violence in the context opened by that book.

It should be acknowledged that whatever the various blandishments of the new Muslim regime, since it is not particularly violent, and its spokesman and president, Mohammed ben-Abbes, disposes of a genuinely reassuring eloquence, the novel's plot is explicit on the repressive thread that holds it together. It revolves around the career of the protagonist: his dismissal from the Sorbonne, which is now lavishly financed by Saudi-Arabia, because he is not Muslim; and then his eventual reintegration into the faculty of the newly Islamicized Sorbonne once he submits and converts. For *Soumission* is the story of a religious conversion promising "the chance of a second life, stripped of any particular connection with the previous one." (299)

Now on the path to conversion, the key juncture turns out to be one in which our professor allows himself to be seduced by the offer tendered to him to edit the de luxe edition of a Pléiade volume devoted to the works of his preferred author, Huysmans. Religious conversion, reintegration into the Islamicized Sorbonne, and the authoring of the "best text ever written on Huysmans" (282), a preface to the Pléiade volume thanks to which he has the "sudden conviction that he understands the totality of Huysmans better than he [Huysmans] understood himself": such are the motifs that fuse and allow the novel to know an ironically happy *dénouement*.

Consider now that the religious conversion, not of Houellebecq's protagonist (to Islam), but of Huysmans, his preferred author, to Catholicism, a delineation of the "unconsciousness" or "unconscious" that serves virtually as the medium through which that conversion is achieved (since Huysmans is said to have understood his work less well than Houellebecq's protagonist would), is the focus of another preface on the subject of Huysmans, the one that Huysmans himself placed at the head of a re-edition of *A rebours* and called his "preface written twenty years after the novel." It deals with the "unconscious" trajectory (Huysmans' word) which brought him from *A rebours* [in 1884] to a conversion to *Catholicism* in 1895. In point of fact, the author tells us, that period is divided in two: a first period (1884-1891) that was "*parfaitement inconscient(e)*," *perfectly unconscious*, up until the novel *Là-bas*, and a second period that was only more or less so…

Such then are the three nodes around which *Soumission* or the literary configuration forming the context of the Parisian attacks of January 2015 were organized: Huysmans, conversion, and the unconscious. Along with, of course, the major difference or reversal that the conversion, which was no less felicitous than Huysmans' to Catholicism, was this time, in *Soumission*, to Islam.

Now it happens that about thirty years ago, on the occasion of the centenary of *A rebours*, I had written an essay on the afterlife of that same novel and which I called "Huysmans: Conversion, Hysteria, and the French 'Unconscious.'" There, then, already, were the three nodes of Houellebecq's novel or of the preface written twenty years after *A rebours*—plus "Hysteria." But the inclusion of "hysteria" in the configuration implied the name of Freud or rather the debate on the meaning of hysteria—and its relation to demonic possession—that divided Freud and Charcot, his Parisian master, on the subject and to whose lectures on "la grande hystérie" there is a significant allusion in *Là-bas*, the Satanic or Satanizing novel of 1891, which year was a turning point in Huysmans' path to conversion… Might Huysmans have attended the same lecture-demonstrations of Charcot at the Salpêtrière as Freud? Houellebecq, in any event, does not fail to forge a link between the two. An evocation of the preface written twenty years after the novel is preceded by an allusion to cancer of the jaw, which was the cause of death of both Huysmans and (years later) Freud.

Hysteria, moreover, brings us to the heart of the more radically "unconscious" period of Huysmans' *oeuvre*, as evoked by the author himself, the one stretching from 1884 to 1891. At the beginning, in *A rebours*, we find the "nodal point," or *Knotenpunkt*—to use a term of Freud's on the interpretation of dreams—which sees the protagonist, des Esseintes, murmuring lines from Mallarmé's poem "Hérodiade" in front of a canvas by Gustave Moreau, a painting of Salome (another name of Hérodiade), then, dancing before the Oriental potentate Herod against the backdrop of a gloriously Byzantine palace.

The Salome motif, then, is a crux in the hyper-aestheticized existence of des Esseintes. Moreover Salome is characterized allegorically in the same novel by Huysmans as "the goddess of immortal Hysteria." But let us move now to the next phase in Huysmans' itinerary, the novel *En rade*, meaning *Stranded* or *A Haven*, which dates from 1887, that is, from the very core of what the author calls the "incubatory" or radically unconscious stage of his work. That novel, *En rade*, which is virtually without a plot, recounts the abjection of a petit-bourgeois Parisian surviving on the brink of bankruptcy and seeking shelter in the dilapidated provincial château of relatives interested above all in robbing him blind. Now the prose of that novel, *En rade*, has the idiosyncratic feature of being periodically invaded (or infiltrated) by a series of dreams or nightmares. The first of these presents us with a striking virgin offering herself to an aged and lubricious Oriental potentate whose stare *vrilla—drilled its way*—into the childlike nudity of the girl, the entire scene taking place against a backdrop of Byzantine flamboyance. In an initial phase, Huysmans' protagonist fails to understand his dream, but the reader of *A rebours*, of course, recognizes (or believes he recognizes) the image of Salome, allegory of Hysteria, and Herod, which would decidedly be an obsession of the author.

And then the reader discovers that he got things wrong. The virgin confronting the potentate in the dream is not Salome confronting Herod in the New Testament but, we are told, rather Esther confronting Ahasuerus in the Old Testament, that is, provoking the execution not of John the Baptist, but of Haman meditating his genocide of the Jews. Salome would be the screen, so to speak, masking Esther and the extermination—or near-extermination—of the Jews. Let us now follow a bit summarily a series of associations in the novel (and which I have developed more amply in my own preface, so to speak, to Huysmans—in which I believed, to speak like Houellebecq's protagonist in *Soumission*, that I had understood things, in the fullness of time, better than Huysmans himself). A tour of the decrepit château of *En rade* reveals to the protagonist a fragrance that begins to obsess him and a fantasy which it inspires and infuses. The somewhat sickening fragrance is of ether, *éther* in the French. But *éther*, with its acute accent replacing the letter *s*, is virtually a French transcription of the name *Esther*. And the fantasy which it infuses is that of human flesh posthumously recycled as fragrance, "the sublimated essences of the dead," specifically the fragrance of soap or *pommades*, ointments.

Might there have been a future of Huysmans' *oeuvre* that took the form of Nazi iconography—flesh into soap—at its most *kitsch*? We take an additional step forward... Next stop is the novel of 1891, *Là-bas*, the culmination of the most "unconscious" or "incubatory" phase of Huysmans' conversion. Là-bas is a Satanical novel undertaken in quest of a mood beyond the mediocrity of modernity and which searches for it in a cult devoted to a monster of medieval legend, Gilles de Rais. Durtal, the protagonist of Huysmans' novel, imagines tonic possibilities of intensity, energy, and health freed up by the monstrous Gilles, as he gives himself over to orgies of abduction, rape, and the murder of young boys in his château of Tiffauges.

Leaping carefully forward now, we arrive at the highly admired novel of Michel Tournier, *Le roi des aulnes*, literally: *The Erl-King* (as in Goethe), but also *The Ogre*. It won the Goncourt Prize in 1970, the heyday of what has been called the Vichy Syndrome. Its subject is the sexual liberation of a Frenchman named Abel Tiffauges in a Nazi youth camp in Germany where he has been assigned to work as a collaborator during the Second World War. From Gilles de Rais's château of Tiffauges to the Nazi training camp in which Abel Tiffauges labors joyfully, the link is solid. But it does little more than pursue the sequence of associations beginning in *A rebours* and leading us transversally via Huysmans' conversion from Esther and the fantasy of a massacre of the Jews to the sickening fragrance of *éther* (or ether) to soaps and ointments laced with human scent and to Gilles de Rais, lord of Tiffauges and "des Esseintes of the fifteenth century." Des Esseintes, it will be recalled, was the name of the protagonist of *A rebours*. Gilles de Rais was also known familiarly as Barbe-bleue, Blue Beard. But such, we also learn, was the name Tournier and his protagonist, Tiffauges, give to Tiffauges's horse or "barbary steed." The coherence of our web continues to grow in density.

**

On a more personal note, I am inclined to state that my effort to posit an afterlife, or hidden center to Huysmans' *oeuvre* in the horrors of the Second World War, might well stem from my never quite having gotten over the enigma constituted by the work of Maurice Blanchot, its investment in metaphors of terror, and the relation between those metaphors and Blanchot's call to terrorism against Jews and communists during the years before the Second World War. It is an enigma which I wrote about in the 1970s, inspired in part by the work of Zeev Sternhell. It earned me a significant number of attacks at the time, and since then a significant number of declarations of solidarity. (I think in particular of Michel Surya's recent volume, which concludes that Blanchot spent years of his life attempting to shore up a number of less than true statements he sent to me in a letter of 1979.)[1] It is as though at a certain point in my life, a relation to what remained unthinkable in the war was the enigma all literary works (and especially French ones) owed it to themselves to confront.

From Huysmans to Tournier (and *Le roi des Aulnes*), then. But it is a link which is no more strange, after all, than the bridge between Huysmans and Houellebecq sketched or achieved in *Soumission*. The British writer Julian

---

1 See Michel Surya, *L'autre Blanchot: L'écriture de jour, l'écriture de nuit* (Paris: Gallimard, 2015, p. 97: "Blanchot paraît par là donner raison à l'argument central, et quoi qu'on ait dit, imparable, de Mehlman (auquel "Les intellectuels en question" constitue pour partie une réponse cryptée)…"

Barnes, moreover, has stated that Houellebecq was potentially the most sub-stantial novelist to surface in France since Tournier (*New Yorker*, July 7, 2003).

Might there be a bridge between those two bridges? It is a question to which we shall return. The conversion of the protagonist of *Soumission* is registered against a certain resistance (and the weakness of such resistance may be one of the principal points of the novel). But the price to be paid for rein-tegration into the faculty of a newly Islamicized Sorbonne will be just such a conversion. The discussion over the terms of François's conversion with Redi-ger, former leader of a campaign to boycott Israeli universities and head of the new Sorbonne, will be difficult, but is facilitated to some extent by a bottle of chilled "white wine bearing the label 'Meursault'." It will be recalled that the honor of Meursault, which is the name of Camus's *étranger* or "stranger," lay, toward the end of Camus's narrative, in not allowing himself to be convinced or converted by the prison chaplain. In Houellebecq's novel, Meursault is the name of the lubricant that allows a conversion—to Islam—to *take place*. Such would be one measure of the new decadence of French literature.

The negotiation will take place in the home of the President of the Sorbonne, his address being 5 rue des Arènes. It is an address vaguely familiar to the protagonist, a professor of letters, because Jean Paulhan, *éminence grise* of French letters during the interwar period, lived at that same address. No place, that is, could be better suited to hosting the evaluation of a projected Pléiade edition—the gold standard—of the complete works of Huysmans than premises formerly occupied by Paulhan. Gradually, however, we discover that what fascinates the protagonist is less Paulhan than his mistress, Dominique Aury, who, under the pen name Pauline Réage, had written the masterpiece of erotic masochism titled *Histoire d'O* (The Story of O). But to say masochism is to say submission. The erotic component of Islam, at least in Houellebecq's novel, would thus be a submission of female to male, the model of a submission of man to God…

So I found myself wondering: was Dominique Aury, alias Pauline Réage, being proposed by Houellebecq as our guide to the erotic subtext gov-erning his imaginary empire of Islam? And then one day I opened up the huge new biography of Dominique Aury and had the shock of discovering in it a chapter titled "Jeffrey Mehlman, 'Blanchot à *Combat*.'" (*Combat* was the name of the journal in which Blanchot issued his call to acts of terror against Jews and

Communists in 1936.) The reason for the title of that chapter of the biography of Dominique Aury is rather surprising, but may be summarized as follows: My reading of the political evolution of Blanchot had insisted on the sequence of two prominent writers who had successively oriented Blanchot in his political thinking early in his career: in the 1930s, Thierry Maulnier, ex-secretary to Charles Maurras, head of *Action* française, had exercised his influence on a Blanchot close to fascism; and then, during the war years, it was rather Jean Paulhan, an intellectual leader of the Resistance, whose influence over Blanchot proved decisive. Now it happens that Dominique Aury, the clandestine author of *Histoire d'O*, had two great clandestine romances in her life (according to her biographer): first, Thierry Maulnier, and subsequently Jean Paulhan. And those two loves coincided with the political influence of those two figures on Blanchot, with whom she maintained a correspondence. With the result that Angie David, the biographer of Dominique Aury, had concluded that I had (perhaps unwittingly) furnished a kind of skeletal outline of Dominique Aury's life in the form of an essay on the political evolution of Blanchot. Blanchot, the literary figure whose split sensibility—from the early association with Action française to what Levinas called "the passivity beyond all passivity" of *l'espace littéraire*—was in some ways responsible for my reading of Huysmans and the afterlife of his *oeuvre*, had furnished an explanatory key to the life of the author, Dominique Aury, of a major novel on the erotics of submission (*Histoire d'O*) and thus of Houellebecq's novel, *Soumission*, itself.

From Huysmans to Tournier and Nazism, on the one hand, and from Huysmans to Houellebecq and Islamic violence on the other. What remains constant, in however different a manner, is violence visited on the Jews. In Tournier, the pleasures of a Nazi youth camp manage virtually to repress any perception of Jewish victimage, which surfaces only at the novel's end and in a manner that is barely convincing. In Houellebecq, the Jews silently begin to vacate the scene of the novel. More specifically, Myriam, the protagonist's mistress, leaves France for Israel. A conviction that "something quite serious is about to happen in France regarding the Jews" hovers, however discreetly, over the novel. And that thing seems to have occurred at the Hypercacher market a few days after the publication of Houellebecq's novel.

**

Such then—starting with Huysmans and his various heirs (Tournier, Houellebecq), and ending in the bang, not the whimper, of the attack on *Charlie Hebdo* and the kosher market of January 2015—is the state of the question of literature and violence in France. Moreover, it is an ending that has not left what preceded it quite intact. Which is why I will end these remarks with an observation on the changing status of one of the primordial works of French literature, Proust's great novel, and its shifting status under the pressure of the emblematic ending—Houellebecq's novel—just evoked.

There is an origin of Proust's novel that is transmitted in the celebrated episode of the good night kiss scene, constituting as it does a kind of official story of the genesis of the author's character and his work. Allow me to conclude with some personal comments on how its originary status figures in my own work. They will take us to the re-edited Pléiade edition of Proust's work, which I would juxtapose with the imaginary Pléiade edition of Huysmans at the center of Houellebecq's *Soumission*.

During the celebrated good night kiss scene, in which the narrator's deficient will power emerges as the defining trait of his character, his father, just before yielding catastrophically to his son's wish not to be separated from his mother, is seen with his turban of a night cap as he mounts the stairs to his bedroom. His garb, we are told, resembles that of Biblical Abraham in a *gravure* by the Renaissance painter Benozzo Gozzoli. In it he is seen instructing Sarah to take her distance from their son Isaac, presumably in preparation for the sacrificial and arch-patrilinear episode known as the "binding of Isaac." The irony, which is deliberate and huge, is that Marcel's father, despite his resemblance to Abraham, fails to implement that crucial separation between mother and son which was Abraham's signal achievement. The repercussions of that failure—from the decisive decline of Marcel's will to the redemptive capacity of *involuntary* memory (with one absence of will redeeming the other) and the twin "accursed races," Jews and inverts, joined in the longest simile in the entire novel, in the volume significantly titled *Sodome et Gomorrhe*—are all elements crucial to an understanding of Proust. And such was the reading of Proust that I attempted in the first chapter of my doctoral dissertation, which bears an epigraph plucked from Kafka: "*Ich könnte mir einen anderen Abraham denken* (I could imagine another or different Abraham)."

Now the recent re-edition of the Pléiade Proust contains a striking footnote to the Abraham image we are attending to. Its principal point is that the scene , bidding Sarah to stay away from Isaac (in anticipation of his sacrifice) was never actually painted by Benozzo Gozzoli (in his Pisan series of scenes from the life of Abraham), nor does it, for that matter, occur per se in Genesis. Moreover, the closest the philological record comes to the scene—with mother and son—invoked by Proust is Abraham instructing Hagar to rejoin her son (*à se départir du côté de*) Ishmael in his impending exile. It is as though the Proustian image of Abraham, betrayed by the narrator's father in the novel, was originally and already the result of a deformation of the saga of Hagar and Ishmael—which is to say, in a complicated way—of Islam. There would be, in sum, beyond the Biblical patriarch, at least two *other* Abrahams: Proust's defective patriarch and Benozzo Gozzoli's, which just happens to have been destroyed during World War II.

Moreover, the footnote is, at some level, philologically sound. Consider the expression *se départir du côté de*. It could plainly mean taking a distance or parting from the side of…, but also *taking a distance or parting in the direction of…*. The first case would separate mother (Sarah) from Isaac and Abraham; the second would separate mother (Hagar) and Ishmael from Abraham. For *du côté de* can mean both toward and away from, to and fro. And as if wittingly or unwittingly chiming in on the subject, Proust himself, of course, just happened to give to the first volume of his vast novel the title *Du côté de chez Swann*. (It is a title which, in its full deconstructive coherence, one is tempted to write "*Du cóté de" chez Swann*—i.e., the undecidable phrase in the home of Swann, the Jew…).

The second Pléiade Proust, in sum, suggests, at the core of the novel, an original injustice done to Islam (Ishmael), an unwitting deformation of that victimization in the form of a commandment central to Jewish identity (the *Akedah*), and an ironically intended betrayal of that very commandment in the form of an abdication by the narrator's father at a key juncture of the novel. One is inclined to say that this Proust seems ready-made for study in the Islamicized Sorbonne, lavishly funded by Saudi-Arabia, of Houellebecq's novel. It is situated where the *fictive* Pléiade of *Soumission*, dedicated to Huysmans, and with its concomitant exclusion of Jews from the study of French literature, meets up with the *actual* Pléiade of Proust, but it is also, the memorialist in me wants to say, where the "other Abraham" with which my dissertation—that is, my career, at its inception—meets up with a reading of Houellebecq's penultimate novel, published on the day of an assault against freedom of expression, ultimately against literature, from which the French have yet to recover.

8

Marcel Mauss and the French "Unconscious"

In 2008, just prior to his hundredth birthday, an immortality of sorts was conferred on the anthropologist Claude Lévi-Strauss when his *Oeuvres* were published—leather-bound, gold-embossed, on Bible paper —in Gallimard's Pléiade collection. He died the following year and we have since begun to see, for the first time, assessments of his achievement—including the two volumes under review in these pages —in a world without Lévi-Strauss.[1] Patrick Wilcken's stylishly written biography is considerably shorter than Denis Bertholet's French biography of 2003, but is nonetheless the first in a position to take in the entire arc of the anthropologist's career—from his nineteenth-century-style expeditions to the Brazilian interior in the 1930s, via his wartime exile in New York, where the twin influences of the linguist Roman Jakobson and assorted Surrealists led to the writing of a ground-breaking thesis, to the vanguard structuralist project, the international celebrity, the eventual disillusionment with modernism, the unexpected late references to Gobineau (from an anti-racist ideologue), and the final years, when he claimed to feel like a "shattered hologram" and received the visit of a notoriously philistine President of France on his hundredth birthday. Wilcken steers his biography skillfully between the pitfalls of reverence and dismissiveness. It is useful, for instance,

---

1 The books reviewed are Patrick Wilcken, *Claude Lévi-Strauss: The Poet in the Laboratory* (New York: Penguin, 2010) and Vincent Debaene, *L'adieu au voyage: L'ethnologie française entre science et littérature* (Paris: Gallimard, 2010).

to be reminded by a skeptical John Updike that "with such a hunting license granted, parallels and homologies are easy to bag—child's play for a brain as agile as M. Lévi-Strauss (299)." But it is equally good to learn of the frequency with which what Wilcken calls Lévi-Strauss' "hit-and-run tactics" would pay-off, generating fresh perspectives (75).

The biography is particularly good at situating Lévi-Strauss's work in an Anglo-American context. The anthropologist's polemical letters against the translator of *La Pensée sauvage*, Sybil Wolfram, who gave as good as she got, are as revealing as they are painful. As is the about-face of one-time disciple Rodney Needham, who ultimately turned against the "unreliability" of Lévi-Strauss' "on-the-hoof ideas-driven method," a circumstance that earned him an attack by the author in a last-minute preface to *Elementary Kinship Structures*, which Needham himself had translated. Beyond that, it is helpful, in contextualizing structuralism, to be served such English-language references as Robert Hughes on cubism ("all relationships, a twinkling field of interrelated events") and Alex Ross on the "Cold War laboratory-experiment aesthetic" of postwar avant-garde music (227, 245). Finally, the strength of Wilcken's book lies less in any new information provided than in the author's ability never to lose contact with the sensibility behind Lévi-Strauss' effort and the metaphors best able to convey it: from the affinity for "similarities between sets of differences" to myth as a Calder-inspired mobile or, better yet, as a crystal growing "spiral-wise" until the impulse that produced it is exhausted… (235, 257).

Vincent Debaene's sprawling *L'adieu au voyage: L'ethnologie française entre science et littérature* is an altogether different affair. Debaene is an editor of the Pléiade edition of Lévi-Strauss and a professor of French literature at Columbia University, at whose faculty club, during the War, Lévi-Strauss sustained the shock, at lunch, of witnessing the collapse and death of Franz Boas, from whom, he said, "all of American anthropology issued" (138). Debaene's volume is an impressively erudite exercise in literary and intellectual history. A third (and final) division of the book ranges far and wide on the issue of French literature's vexed relations with the human sciences—from Durkheim's sociology and the Catholic, right-wing reaction to its usurpation of literature's claims to wisdom at the beginning of the twentieth century to a polemical configuration complicated by the fact that Lévi-Strauss' prose style was deemed to resemble nothing so much as that of the *ur*-romantic Chateaubriand. But the heart of the book is an effort to forge for literary history the genre that culminates in the anthropologist's classic memoir of 1955, *Tristes tropiques*, and it is that principal focus that is most deserving of attention.

Consider first the specific mournfulness at the heart of the *tristes tropiques* that give a name to Lévi-Strauss' book. It famously relates to a history of failed encounters between Europe and America, an ongoing fiasco attributable to the fact that such engagements have invariably occurred either too early or too late. On the one hand, an encounter with a pristine America that Europe, in its anthropological naïveté, was in no way equipped to assess. On the other, a confrontation with an America thoroughly contaminated by Europe, an object that might be amenable to understanding by a Europe at last adequate to the task were it not for the fact that that object was so vitiated in its integrity by years of exploration and exploitation that little remained of it to be understood.

The temporal impasse of engaging the other too early or too late would issue in an attempted solution in the form of what Wilcken calls the "hymn to proportionality" of structuralism (338). The best access to the otherness of the other would be by way of an appreciation of our own otherness to ourselves, that is, via a version of the unconscious that as often as not seems to be a dandified and hyper-syntactical take on the spatial opposition between "too close" and "too far." Thus medieval Perceval, the myth of a male who brings about a "waste land" by being too slow to ask a question, is construed symmetrically as an inversion of ancient Oedipus, the myth of a male who brings about a plague by being too incestuously quick to provide an answer...

To read Debaene's book is for this reader, first of all, to be aware that one is approaching *Tristes tropiques*, a classic of structuralism, in an age that is not merely post-structuralist, but post-post structuralist. It is, that is, to be reminded of the temporal disjunction attendant on Lévi-Strauss' belated encounter in the 1930s with the variously decimated tribes of Brazil. For what strikes one initially is just how much what might be called the homological *frisson* and the specific thrill it could elicit, which for many of us was the *raison d'être* of structuralism, appears to have waned as a writerly impulse even among those whose expertise on Lévi-Strauss is beyond question. Debaene treasures his *Tristes tropiques* and would shield it from what he seems to regard as the cultural junk of "literary structuralism." He takes special pleasure in quoting the master himself on the various "coherent delusions" that litter the cultural landscape of speculative thought under the name of "structuralism" (452). The principal offender appears to be Roland Barthes, severely chastised by Debaene, who accuses him of working at a "thousand leagues' distance from genuine structuralism" (465). (And no doubt, he might savor the episode in Wilcken's biography that sees Lévi-Strauss turning down a request from Barthes that he direct the thesis that became *Le Système de la mode*" [242-243]). Beyond Barthes, and serving as testimony that his book is not so much post-structuralist as post-post-structuralist, Debaene takes pleasure in mocking Derrida: "One might amuse oneself by assembling adverbs of time in Barthes's article or in the contemporary reflections of Derrida: there is a quasi-messianic dimension in the promised advent of *écriture*" (465). Or in ignoring him: For anyone who recalls the polemical tensions generated around Derrida's attempted deconstruction of the "Leçon d'écriture" in *Tristes tropiques*, the fact that a would-be history of *Tristes tropiques*, intent on fully contextualizing it, should omit mention of *De la grammatologie* is stunning.

The contextualization Debaene has in mind is quite different. His focus is the "second" and more autobiographical volume written by a slew of French anthropologists and which together constitute a literary genre unto themselves. These include Alfred Métraux's *Ile de Pâques* (1941), which Bataille considered one of the masterpieces of French literature of the day; Jacques Soustelle's *Mexique, terre indienne* (1936), prefaced by Paul Rivet, founder of the Musée de l'Homme; Marcel Griaule's idiosyncratic *Les Flambeurs d'homme*, which won the Prix Gringoire in 1934; Michel Leiris's monument to the futility of travel, *L'Afrique fantôme* (1934), and *Tristes tropiques* itself, viewed as something of the culminating achievement of a tradition constituted, after the fact, around it. By the end of his study, Debaene is able to conclude provocatively—indeed almost deconstructively—that "le deuxième livre," to the extent that it appears to open up unsuspected literary or intellectual possibilities to its author, functions less as a "secondary" text than as a primal or initiatory achievement. And to the extent that the disappointments of *L'Afrique fantôme* (with its insistence on "a small constellation of things that one tends to reproduce, in different forms, an unlimited number of times") make it an experimental laboratory for what would become the first volumes of *La Règle du jeu*, or that *Tristes tropiques* seems pregnant with the future of Lévi-Strauss' structuralism, this is arguably (and intriguingly) the case (275).

But to the extent that the terms invoked to characterize these "second books" entail more often than not an appeal to the "evocativeness" of the "living document," a trend that begins, in *L'adieu au voyage*, with a contemporary description of *Mexique, terre indienne*, as "joining the emotion of the man to the observation of the expert," there is a certain predictability or thinness in the characterization of many of the books evoked (16). Indeed, not even the insistence on the future flowering of *L'Afrique fantôme* in and as *Biffures*, the first volume of *La Règle du jeu*, can quite redeem the tedium of the oft mentioned *ennui* characterizing the traveler's (but also the reader's) experience of Leiris's travel journal. (279, 291).

Leiris and Lévi-Strauss are on several occasions twinned by Debaene as offering a way beyond the consolidation of the ego's experience, beyond the opposition between self and other and toward what might be called a beneficent expropriation in or as the "unconscious." (300, 474) And he is surely right to do so. But the constraints of the doctoral thesis that his book originally was are such that the future glories of *La Règle du jeu* (in the case of Leiris) or of structural analysis, what I have called the homological *frisson* (in that of Lévi-Strauss) are no more than alluded to in passing. Unless, of course, this having been a thesis written in a post-post-structuralist age, they have been forgotten.

Perhaps it is time, in the interest of full disclosure, for the reviewer to confess that he too is the author of a doctoral thesis, submitted more than forty years ago (1971) at Yale University, culminating in a reading of *Tristes tropiques*, and oriented by an intuition of the profound resonance between the efforts of Lévi-Strauss and Michel Leiris. *My Structural Study of Autobiography* is a very different sort of book from Debaene's (which appears to be unaware of its existence, or perhaps has long since consigned it to the dustbin of "literary structuralism"), but it does have one significant element in common with his: a failure to take into account Derrida's critique of the "Writing Lesson" in *Tristes tropiques*.[2] If Debaene's thesis, that is, may have arrived too late on the scene to take an interest in Derrida's chapter on *Tristes tropiques*, mine may have been a case of arriving too early to realize its import. To find oneself, en route to structuralism, between encounters too early and too late, in any event, offers a precise harmonic with the principal temporal configuration of *Tristes tropiques*, and is a spur to pursue

---

2 J. Mehlman, *A Structural Study of Autobiography: Proust, Leiris, Sartre, Lévi-Strauss* (Ithaca: Cornell University Press, 1974).

whatever overtones it may afford. A thesis too early? Debaene had the modesty, in discussing Leiris, to restrict himself to *L'Afrique fantôme*, which emerges as a series of "disappointing" prolegomena to the rich trove of textual ramifications, barely alluded to, in *La Règle du jeu*. (And in restricting himself to his announced subject, the "second books" of a number of anthropologists, he was certainly right to do so.) In New Haven 1971, I felt no compunction about pursuing the richest literary deposits to be found in Leiris—to wit, the various transformations of the chain that took him from "Perséphone" to "perce-oreille" to "phonographe." Indeed the riches to be culled from *La Règle du jeu*, deliberately neglected by Debaene, were irresistibly such as to occasionally remind me of an early critique of the style of reading I felt myself to be trying out and which was described by Roger Shattuck as so much "strip-mining." Which would place my all too early encounter with Lévi-Strauss fully in harmony with the exploitative cast of the all too early European despoilers of the Americas evoked by Lévi-Strauss as his predecessors in *Tristes tropiques*.

There is, however, a common intertextual link characterizing both efforts, Debaene's and mine, and it involves Proust. Debaene nicely notes a deviation in Lévi-Strauss from an original aspiration to follow in the footsteps of Conrad. As though anthropology's original literary vocation entailed a Polish connection, one that had Malinowski claiming to embark on a journey to the "heart of darkness." The "extreme point of *sauvagerie*" that Lévi-Strauss would engage eventually gives way, at a turning point of the memoir, to an acknowledgment of a fundamental frustration, which is epistemological in nature (316). Standing before the Tupi natives, Lévi-Strauss realizes: "Were I to succeed in no more than divining what they were about, they would be stripped of their foreignness (*étrangeté*); I might just as well have stayed in my village. Or, were they to retain it, as in this case, it would be of no use to me, since I would not even be able to grasp what makes it foreign."[3] Such is what Debaene, in his chapter on Proust, calls the "impasses of empiricism," the impossibility of knowing the other as other. But what he shies away from developing is the intuition that precisely that epistemological bind is what spells the doom of romantic love in Proust. Lévi-Strauss stands before the Tupi natives, that is, much as Swann does before Odette. For the Proustian passion was to know the

---

3 Claude Lévi-Strauss, *Tristes tropiques* (Paris: Plon 1955).

unknown woman *as unknown.* And Swann's eventual knowledge of Odette's life coincides with the death of his passion for her. The comparison is thematically grotesque but homologically (i.e., structurally) precise, and it is precisely one that Debaene resists engaging. Instead he retreats to a comparison, nicely developed, between two set pieces: one is the famous passage in which changing perspectives on the steeples of Martinville serve, in Proust, as the pretext for the narrator to try himself out as a *prosateur,* and the other Lévi-Strauss' bravura prose evocation of a sunset at sea, which, in its phenomenological richness, is as far from structuralism as might be imagined.

There is, to be sure, a pressure toward structure—beyond the solipsism of Swann in love or the anthropologist confronting his natives —in *Tristes tropiques.* It may take the form of the hieroglyphics hinting at an as yet inexistent structure of exchange and painted on the faces of the Caduvean women of the Amazon, endowing them with an erotic charge. Or of a moiety system, in the case of the Bororos, that ends up surviving the hierarchical caste system it was forged to conceal. Both cases point to the role of Marcel Mauss, theorist of the mode of reciprocal exchange that would lie at the core of Lévi-Strauss' notion of the structural unconscious. That unconscious, through which the subject partakes in his own otherness to himself, was Lévi-Strauss' key to the communication that might dispel the "impasses of empiricism." It was a realm intuited by Mauss, according to Lévi-Strauss, who figures, in the anthropologist's "Introduction à l'oeuvre de Marcel Mauss," as a "Moses leading his people up to a promised land whose splendor he would never contemplate."[4] Lévi-Strauss' structuralism would lie in a forcing of what was merely implicit, received but not articulated, in the works of Marcel Mauss.

Which brings us unexpectedly back to Proust. On August 19, 1916, Durkheim, who will play a significant role in Debaene's book, sent a letter to Marcel Mauss, his nephew, from the beach at Cabourg, the model of Proust's Balbec. The salutation reads: "Mon cher Marcel…" The letter's closing reads: "The beach is encumbered (*encombrée*) with Jews. I know more than thirty Semites of every sex (*trente sémites de tout sexe*) in Cabourg…"[5] After Cabourg (or Balbec), Combray (*encombrée*), followed by a reduction of the longest simile

---

4 Lévi-Strauss, "Introduction à l'oeuvre de Marcel Mauss" in Marcel Mauss, *Sociologie et anthropologie* (Paris: Presses Universitares de France, 1950), p. 37.
5 Emile Durkheim, *Lettres à Marcel Mauss* (Paris: Presses Universitaires de France, 1998), p. 544.

in the novel: "sémites de tout sexe" or the twinned "cursed races" (in *Sodome et Gomorrhe*) of Jews and/as "inverts." All transmitted to a "cher Marcel." Mauss appears to have been the unwitting or unconscious recipient (from Durkheim via what Lévi-Strauss would call the avunculate) of a summary (or, in 1916, an anticipation) of Proust's novel. And it is precisely the imperative of introducing Mauss's "unconscious" at the turning point in *Tristes tropiques* that finds Lévi-Strauss helplessly confronting the Tupis, in an epistemological homologue of the predicament of the doomed lover in Proust. From which miniature of Proust's novel, in a letter that has interested us not at all for its content, but solely for its frame (salutation, heading, and closing), we would derive or purloin—to use a favorite word of Lévi-Strauss' friend, Jacques Lacan —the essence of Proust's novel.

Cabourg encombrée/Balbec-en-Combray: the space of the letter received by Mauss, even beyond questions of plot (i.e., its "Semites of every sex"), is like a dreamt conflation of the principal loci of Proust's novel. But *encombrée* deserves to be read as well as a reminder that the key to the "unconscious" that Lévi-Strauss would derive from Mauss is the notion of the "floating signifier," precisely what, in the case of Durkheim's letter from the beach, binds *Tristes tropiques* to Proust's novel.

We are not yet done with Mauss' correspondence as it impinges on the labyrinthine subject of Debaene's book. For we shall see that one of the most striking passages in the volume involves nothing other than a fragment of a letter *from* Mauss in June 1938, and its resonances in the years that would follow. The circumstance is as follows. The central section of *L'adieu au voyage* deals with three "exceptional" books: *Tristes tropiques*, as we know, is the central focus of Debaene's volume and is on more than one occasion paired with *L'Afrique fantôme* and its role in preparing the astonishing post-egological pages of *La Règle du jeu*. But it is concerning the third book, Marcel Griaule's *Les Flambeurs d'hommes*, that Debaene brings his most interesting news. Griaule, a student of Mauss, was the leader of the pioneering Dakar-Djibouti mission to Ethiopia from 1931 to 1933. It was an expedition on which he was in fact accompanied by Leiris (with whom he later broke over Leiris' denunciation of the wholesale seizure of archeological artifacts for non-scientific ends.) *Les Flambeurs d'hommes* relates the tribal punishment of an alleged assassination attempt by setting the culprit, wrapped in mosquito netting swathed in hot wax, aflame in public (243). Griaule's reaction is worth noting: "A vision of Hell, the expression is not too strong: it will be conceded that in an atmosphere of such exaltation it is enough for a flame emitted by a man to reach five meters in height for it to appear infernal."[6] Of Debaene's comments on Griaule's book, the most striking is that the episode of the human torch is, in fact, a shameless invention. In addition, there is the "enunciatory strangeness" of the book, a memoir written in the third person, and the fact of the author's scandalous empathy with the brutality he portends to convey (252). Before long, Debaene has opened up a lengthy "digression" on what he calls "Sociology and Cruelty." It is the most interesting section of the book.

"Sociologie et cruauté," prompted by the legend of the "people-burners" of Abyssinia, feels like a regression to the Conradian identification of the Malinowski tradition in anthropology. But in fact Debaene makes a literary connection between Griaule's book and Stendhal's *Chroniques italiennes*, a pseudo-history of Renaissance Italy as reported in a doctored chronicle of unusual violence. The Stendhal who would eventually derive *La Chartreuse de Parme* from the *Chroniques italiennes*, would be to *Les Flambeurs d'hommes* what Proust is to *Tristes tropiques*. But the Stendhal connection, with its investment in a kind of pre-civilized anarchy or savagery, was bound to enter into contact with the cult of the human "beast" as elaborated by Italian fascism. It is not coincidental that the principal historian of Stendhal's evolution from the *Chroniques italiennes* to *La Chartreuse*, who is cited by Debaene, is Maurice Bardèche, a notorious fascist apologist and Holocaust denier. In Debaene's vision, Griaule, then, would substitute Ethiopia, about to be invaded by fascist Italy, for Stendhal's "pre-civilized" Italy, the novelistic world that would eventually give us a Mosca, in *La Chartreuse*, doing his best to earn the nickname of "Cruel."[7]

As the analysis progresses, Debaene brings things into contact with Griaule's palpable contempt for the petty bureaucrats of the League of Nations, his assumption of pedagogical duties in ethnology at the Sorbonne under the Vichy regime, and provocative observations by Michel Beaujour to the effect, concerning Leiris in the 1930s, that the ambiguity of the times was such that a "fascist virtuality" seemed part of the very air breathed by intellectuals. Where-

---

6 Marcel Griaule, *Les Flambeurs d'hommes* (Paris: Calmann-Lévy, 1934), p. 126.

7 Stendhal, *The Charterhouse of Parma*, translated by Margaret Shaw (London, Penguin, 1958), p. 403.

upon he confronts us with a little known and stunning letter of 22 June 1938 from Marcel Mauss to his sometime student Roger Caillois. After praising Caillois for his interpretation of the myth of the praying mantis, he offers the following criticism: "As for your general biology, it calls for the strongest reservations […] what I believe to be a general insanity (*déraillement*) of which you yourselves are victims, that kind of absolute irrationalism with which you end up, in the name of the labyrinth and of Paris, the modern myth—but I think that all of you right now are [its victims], probably under the influence of Heidegger, a Bergsonian tarrying in the orbit of Hitler, legitimizing a Hitlerianism infatuated with irrationalism —, and above all the kind of political philosophy you attempt to derive from it in the name of poetry and a vague sentimentality. As much as I am convinced that poets and men of great eloquence can occasionally impose a rhythm on social life, I am to a similar degree skeptical as to the capacities of any philosophy, and above all a philosophy of Paris, to provide a rhythm for anything at all."[8] Caillois was, of course, Leiris' associate at the Collège de sociologie, and the third member of the collective *tous* whom Mauss appears to be designating in his misgivings about the influence of a Nazified Heidegger, as Debaene notes, is surely Georges Bataille. Nor was Mauss alone, it should be noted, in his worries about where Caillois seemed to be heading in 1938. Reacting to Caillois's essay "L'aridité" at the time, Walter Benjamin confessed his fascination with the Frenchman in a letter to Horkheimer, but characterized him as at bottom a Balzacian *arriviste*, an intellectual Rastignac to whom it had befallen to reckon with the "Goebbels clique" rather than the oligarchy of the Faubourg Saint-Germain.[9] (But then Mauss' warnings about the limits of the political validity of what he calls a "philosophy of Paris" might just as well have applied to Benjamin's *Arcades Project* as to Caillois' "Paris, mythe moderne"). Benjamin, of course, would end up a suicidal victim of Hitler's persecution on the Spanish border, and Caillois a Gaullist ideologue of Resistance in Argentina, but the terms of the critiques offered by Mauss and Benjamin have the cumulative effect of sketching a virtuality that meshes nicely (or disquietingly) with the tutelary role ascribed to Griaule's *Les Flambeurs d'hommes*

---

8 Marcel Mauss, "Lettre à Roger Caillois" [1938], *Actes de la recherche en sciences sociales*, No. 84, September 1990, p. 87.

9 Unpublished letter of May 28, 1938, quoted in Theodor W. Adorno and Walter Benjamin, *The Complete Correspondence* (Cambridge: Harvard University Press, 1999), p. 275.

by Debaene. Small wonder that Griaule should assume the chair in ethnology under Vichy's governance of the Sorbonne.

For all its commercial success, Griaule's "second book" receives rather harsh treatment from Debaene. He describes it as lacking "minimal coherence" and affirms: "*Les Flambeurs d'hommes* is not a good work of scholarship (*un bon livre savant*)" (265, 268). This is sufficiently the case to set the reader wondering why it retains the crucial role it does in his study. For it should not be forgotten that the center of Debaene's voyage to his melancholy anthropological hell consists, in fact, of three concentric circles: at dead center, *Tristes tropiques*; then, twinned with it, the "disappointing reading" of *L'Afrique fantôme*; and finally, Griaule's fictive (and incoherent) holocaust of human body-burning. Might the architectonic role attributed to it be a response to other constraints than its strict anthropological importance? It is here that the digression on "sociology and cruelty" with its remarkable extended quotation from Mauss' letter to Caillois, the prospective Hitlerian (who would end up a Gaullist), deserves closer attention.

Caillois surfaces to interesting effect in Wilcken's biography, where we learn that he had gone head-to-head with Lévi-Strauss in competition for Mauss' old chair, which Lévi-Strauss ended up securing. When one recalls that Lévi-Strauss' way out of the impasses of empiricism was by way of dislodging the concept of the unconscious which he had already located in Mauss' *Essai sur le don* at a turning point in *Tristes tropiques*, situating himself as the heir to the "Moses" of the promised land of structuralism, one begins to understand the ferocity of the polemic between Caillois and Lévi-Strauss. In 1954, Caillois, editor of *Diogène*, accused Lévi-Strauss of perversely exaggerating the achievements of primitive cultures in a two-part review of *Race et histoire* in *La Nouvelle Revue française*.[10] Lévi-Strauss responded with unexpected polemical violence in a piece, titled "Diogène couché," in *Les Temps modernes* (1955). The piece survives largely because of a single line: "America had its Mc Carthy, and we have our McCaillois." The implication was that Caillois was a dangerous apologist for the West.

Our reason for concentrating on Caillois, it will be recalled, is that he is the focus of the most striking passage in the most idiosyncratic section of *L'adieu au voyage:* Mauss' epistolary warning in 1938 to Caillois and his associ-

10 Roger Caillois, "Illusion à rebours" in *La Nouvelle revue française*, nos. 24-25, December 1954 (pp. 1010-1024)-January 1955 (pp. 58-70).

ates (*"vous…tous"*), cited in the context of Debaene's digression on sociology and cruelty, that they were straying in dangerous proximity to a Heidegger already in the orbit of Hitler. The associates of Caillois in 1938 were preeminently Georges Bataille and Leiris, cofounders with him of the Collège de sociologie. But to recall as much is immediately to recall that Lévi-Strauss and Bataille were crucially champions of very different interpretations of Mauss' essay on *Le Don*: on the one hand, Lévi-Strauss and reciprocal, almost homeostatic, exchange—of women —as the principle of social stability; on the other, Bataille and potlatch as a ruinous principle of competitive expenditure or destruction viewed as the transgressive core of humanity itself. One could write a whole history of recent French thought (at least in its structuralist and post-structuralist phases) in terms of the divided legacy of Marcel Mauss.

The Caillois-Lévi-Strauss polemic was curiously enduring in its ambivalence. Lévi-Strauss eventually invited Caillois to deliver the address welcoming him to the French Academy when he was narrowly elected in 1974. The address turned out to be a protracted critique. As quoted by Wilcken: "The structural method does not escape from the social sciences' original sin, which is to move little by little from plausible conjecture to a kind of inexcusable reductiveness, infallible in all circumstances…It seems to me, however, that doubt has never ceased to torment you [i.e., Lévi-Strauss]. You have been less and less inclined to go beyond pure description. You have taken to task those of your followers whose excesses have alarmed you. You have been frightened by the expansion of structuralism…" (317). Structuralism: "constantly on the lookout," according to Caillois in his address, "for echoes, reflections, harmonies" assumed to constitute "the framework of the universe"

Perhaps it is time to pause in our review of Debaene's provocative book and recall where it has taken us. On the one hand, we have found ourselves fixated on a letter sent by Durkheim to Mauss in 1916, which we have infused with the distilled essence of Proust's novel, the work that serves as the intertext of the central focus of Debaene's study, *Tristes tropiques*. On the other, the bizarrely charged letter of Mauss to Caillois, written in 1938 and excavated by Debaene, which seems pregnant with what scholars would eventually call the Vichy syndrome. The first letter does not even appear in Debaene's book, but appears to make the argument for the Proust intertext—to discover Proust while mining the legacy of Mauss—as effectively as might be hoped for. The second—the Mauss letter (on and) to a seemingly Nazified Caillois and Company is strikingly lodged in the least expected section of Debaene's volume. For the student of French letters, they together appear to encapsulate with barely imaginable concision an entire swathe of French culture in the twentieth century. In order to perceive them, however, one might have to be on the lookout, to quote the lines of Caillois that many assumed to be a critique, for that sensitivity to "echoes, reflections, and harmonies" that may have been the lasting legacy of Lévi-Strauss and that Debaene's book at its most intriguing invites us to ponder.

9

Schmaltz, Kitsch, and *Context*

The art of criticism is a knack for recontextualization, and one way of gauging the achievement of Paul Reitter in *Bambi's Jewish Roots,* a series of razor-sharp essays on Euro-Judaic culture, each with its attendant revelation, is in terms of the quotient of surprise its essays deliver.[1] Take what is perhaps the most pathos-charged—and, to that extent, central—episode in the annals of contemporary critical theory, the death of Walter Benjamin. His flight from France early in World War II, the anticipation of refuge in New York, a bureaucrat's refusal to allow him to cross the border into Spain, and, finally, the suicide in Port Bou together serve to shield many a practitioner of critical theory from charges of idealism, the solipsistic tinge to which allegory, in the strong sense, might seem vulnerable. On the one hand, Benjamin gloriously doomed; on the other, Benjamin's small cohort (principally the photographer Henny Gurland and her son Joseph), who made it across the Pyrenees to the border, but managed, unlike Benjamin, to cross over and make their way to New York. The tragic hero, then, and his not quite anonymous chorus… It has the kind of pathos that had the author of these pages some years back calling up Joseph Gurland at his office at Brown University, where rumor had it that he was still teaching, only to conclude that the most appropriate answer to such a call was the no-answer-at-all that put an end to my attempt to contact him. Or was it the pathos that ended up as a kitsch novel, *Benjamin's Crossing,* by Jay

---

1 *Bambi's Jewish Roots and other Essays on German-Jewish Culture* (Bloomsbury Academic, 2015).

Parini? Or that saw Régis Debray, one of France's great prose stylists, writing the libretto of an opera on Benjamin's "last night" that was first staged by the Opéra de Lyon in 2017?

The suicide and the survivor, then. Except that Henny Gurland appears in Reitter's book in an altogether unexpected context. Shortly after Benjamin's suicide she arrives in New York and marries Erich Fromm, a thinker dismissed by Adorno as a "professional Jew" and the author of *The Art of Loving*, a work disparaged by many a Freudian as half self-help book, half breviary of narcissism. Whereupon the context expands still further. She and Fromm take off to Mexico, where he will live for almost a quarter of a century, tending to his wife's precarious health and leaving a mark on the Mexican Psychoanalytic Society, which he founded. And stranger still, it is she, the legendary survivor of the circumstances leading to Benjamin's self-inflicted death, who would herself commit suicide in Mexico, figuring at some level the mirror of the death that looms so centrally in the legend of the twentieth century intellectual.

Or take a second case that seems structured by the same configuration. Consider the well-known letter of Gershom Scholem to (and against) Hannah Arendt on the "flippancy" of her writing on the Eichmannn trial and the "banality of evil": "In the Jewish tradition there is a concept, hard to define yet concrete enough, which we know as *Ahavat Yisrael*: 'Love of the Jewish people...' In you, dear Hannah, as in so many intellectuals who came from the German Left, I find little trace of this." Now Arendt's critique of the Jewish people in the case of Eichmann was already an echo of her critique of the Jews during the time of the Dreyfus affair. But that opposition (between Scholem and Arendt) is all but deconstructed in another text, the recently published diary of Scholem's adolescence (1913-1919), *Lamentations of Youth*. Hence the entry on June 18, 1919: "For me, the blatant dishonesty practiced by Jews in reporting the pogroms grieves me just as much as the pogrom itself. It's terrible to say, but these people have to embellish reality because it's not yet bad enough for them. In this way they declared the pogroms in Polish cities to be far worse than the Armenian atrocities. They only hurt themselves with such gibberish."[2] Wherein we see that same contempt for the Jews on the subject of their travails as would be famously lamented by Scholem in the case of Arendt, but which is

---

2 Gershom Scholem, *Lamentations of Youth: The Diaries of Youth*, 1913-1919 (Cambridge, Harvard University Press, 2007), p. 303.

this time (i.e., originarily) applicable to the situation of Scholem himself. Might the diary, one finds oneself asking, be the ground of (in)difference from which the very possibility of opposition emerges?

And then there is the opposition between Benjamin and Scholem themselves, the latter a sort of superego in the face of which the former could but register his various failures. These famously include Benjamin's inability to come to terms with Judaism, to learn Hebrew, to make his way to Palestine, to complete a major work of scholarship—as opposed to which we may posit Scholem's apparent impatience with those various failures, uttered from within whatever security had been vouchsafed to him by Judaism. Is it not as though Scholem as superego had *had* it with Benjamin as errant id? Yet to read the diary is to discover a scrambling or collapse of that very opposition. We are confronted with the all too easy to forget fact that Scholem was *younger* than Benjamin and that the latter, in his apparent frivolity, displayed considerably more maturity than a Scholem whose "wholesomeness" could seem curiously naive (230).[3]

For the Scholem of the diaries is far less superego than id, a man in the throes of an "indescribable longing for Walter."[4] He is a man who could describe as "one of the biggest blunders of [his] life the letter in which [he] wrote about a pre-established harmony joining their two lives."[5] On March 17, 1918, having written "I'm not worthy of Walter" a few weeks earlier, Scholem records his "need to write to Walter very, very much." And then there are the unexpected references by Scholem to himself as a "holy swindler."[6] For they seem to place him in a region of inquiry superimposable on that of the "false messiah," Sabbatai Sevi, one of Scholem's principal areas of research. Reitter appears to cast Scholem in the ranks of the antinomian, in the grips of a thematic of "redemption through sin," to use a phrase that gives its gloss to the messianic heresy described at greatest length by the master. And the upshot: "the truth (which is mysticism) wrapped in enlightened garb."[7] This, says Scholem, "is also the way I do it." Ultimately, via the clandestine diary, the figure incarnating Jewish super-ego values turns out to be steeped in what the psycho-

---

3 Ibid., p. 230.
4 Ibid., p. 214.
5 Ibid., p. 252.
6 Ibid., p. 173.
7 Ibid., p. 262.

analyst Jean Laplanche would call its libidinal sources—even as, in the Scholem essay titled "Redemption Through Sin," the Law attains its fulfillment by way of its violation and Enlightenment flourishes as the unwitting legacy of a mystical heresy (Sabbatianism).

The considerable success of Reitter's book is thus concomitant with a triangulation of binary values, even when each of the binary values has long been associated with a triangulation of its own. Whence the deconstruction of the suicide/survivor (Benjamin/Gurland) opposition on the Spanish border; the Scholem/Arendt opposition over the Eichmann trial; and the tension inherent in what has been viewed as the exemplary friendship of Benjamin and Scholem.

But there are other congruent cases that surface in the book. These include the titular instance of Felix Salten, the Zionist who appears to have created the fable of Bambi with the vulnerability of the Jews (and Zionism as a remedy for such vulnerability) in mind. From Reitter's perspective, the sentimentalist Salten was "the Max Brod of *fin-de-siècle* Vienna," and Brod's name was best understood as the pun mobilized in Karl Kraus's formulation, "*Geist* smeared on Brod (or *bread*) is *schmaltz*." (44) Brod, then, is a key station on the road to *kitsch* (as Kundera, in *Testaments Betrayed*, would have it) or *schmaltz*," which may entail that the best corrective to the *schmaltz* of Bambi, and the Jewish question it mediates, lay in the lines of Kafka similarly betrayed by Brod, his putative protector, to whom he addressed them: "most Jews who began writing in German wanted to get away from their Jewishness…but their hind legs were still stuck to the fathers' Jewishness, while the forelegs found no new ground. And the resulting despair served as their inspiration."[8] Reitter's chapter, in which the "Austrian *schmaltz*" of Salten's Bambi ends up assimilated into Disney's "American *kitsch*," opens onto questions broader than the strictly Germanic, as we shall see.

Consider, then, in its broader context, a motif already broached in our first chapter: the *kitsch/schmaltz* question as played out between Kundera (on *kitsch*) and Philip Roth (on *schmaltz*) in the novel he dedicated to Kundera, *The Ghost Writer*. An example of the economy that allows one to understand either author in terms of the other might be encapsulated in the formula: *kitsch* is to

---

8 Ibid., p. 44.

shit (in Kundera) as *schmaltz* is to *schmutz,* i.e., filth, in Roth. In *The Unbearable Lightness of Being,* the falsely or narcissistically idealized unit one delights in betraying is sentimentally Czech-communist and imaginary. The Roth counterpart (in, say, *The Ghost Writer*) is the Jewish family. Betrayal of the unit in its unanimity is in each case a form of virtue. The potential withdrawal from publication (in Roth) of a short story said to be anti-Semitic, like the potential retraction of a text against the Party (in Kundera), is an exemplary form of cowardice. The struggle over whether or not to succumb to such cowardice is haunted in each case by a relation to the myth of Oedipus. And as if to consolidate the congruence between the two novels, each concludes with a chapter alluding in its title to Tolstoy: "Married to Tolstoy" in Roth and "Karenin's Smile" in Kundera…

The congruence between the American Jewish novel (by Roth) and the Czech expatriate novel (by Kundera) leaves the critic in this case with the kind of "co-feeling" (to use Kundera's term for what he also calls "emotional telepathy") that might figure a mode of love beyond identification, on the far side of what Benjamin, who disdained it, called "empathy."

In the spirit of criticism-as-recontextualization, the critic at this juncture is tempted to expand the context of what Reitter has accomplished in his book still further. There is a little noticed but crucially French intrusion into Roth's Kunderian twin text as well. At a key juncture in *The Ghost Writer,* the protagonist's mother enrages her son by tearfully asking him, over the telephone, on the basis of the satiric tone of one of his short stories, whether he is "really anti-Semitic."[9] In an effort to supply an answer to her own question, she tells her son: "When Grandma was dying, you wrote her a letter that was like a poem. It was like—like listening to French, it was so beautiful."[10] Years later, in a protracted interview with Claudia Roth Pierpont, the author supplied a source of sorts for the exchange on Frenchness in the novel: "In a loving letter that he wrote to his maternal 'grandma' from college when she was very ill—his mother would have translated and read it to her—he proudly told her that he had a part in a play (it was the Ragpicker in Giradoux's [*stet*] *The Madwoman of Chaillot*) and described it as 'a very poor man, much like Grandpa must have been when he first saw America. And like you and Grandpa, this poor man

---

9 Philip Roth, *The Ghost Writer* (New York: Vintage, 1979), p. 108.
10 Ibid., p. 107.

wants the world to be good.'" To which Claudia Roth Pierpont adds paren-
thetically: "Roth finds this letter unbearably sentimental today."[11]

The misspelling of Giraudoux's name above perhaps bespeaks the kind
of indifference to the text of the Frenchman's last play, written in Occupied
France during World War II, and that saw Roth eliding any reference to it in
the novel itself. Now *The Madwoman of Chaillot* is to all appearances a less than
typical Giraudoux play. Written in 1943, it is centered on a syndicate of sinister
and racially distinct aliens who had invaded a Parisian neighborhood in the
hope of speculating on the oil deposits believed to lie under the streets of Paris.
They are eventually defeated by a crew of neighborhood zanies, led by the lov-
ably loony Madwoman of Chaillot and the Ragpicker (played by Roth in the
aforementioned letter), who lure the head of the sinister syndicate—called the
President, but elsewhere in Giraudoux's oeuvre superimposable on a character
named Moïse (i.e., Moses)— into a subterranean sewer from which they are
never to return. It is the Ragpicker who is most eloquent on the theme of the
ruinous wartime invasion of Paris by foreign speculators. Which means that
the discourse of Roth-Zuckerman, however "unbearably sentimental" it might
appear, is far more attuned to the treacherous schmutz or filth of anti-Semitism
than to any form of *schmaltz.*

I have already suggested that *The Madwoman of Chaillot* is not in format typical of Giraudoux's theatre. That typical format entails a reversal at the
heart of the text of many a play or myth that reveals just how far from the
truth the received version of many a cultural document is. Now it happens that
Giraudoux's final play may be succinctly situated as a reversal of the scenario
at the heart of *Racine's* final play, *Athalie.* For Athalie was the crazed Biblical
queen (and daughter of Jezabel) intent—for dynastic reasons—on eliminating
the Jews. It is the Jews, however, who eventually triumph over their nemesis by
luring Athalie into a murderous trap of their own. *The Madwoman of Chaillot*,
in sum, deserves to be read as the revenge of Athalie. (Such, moreover, is the
reading of Giraudoux's final play that I have undertaken in *Legacies: Of Anti-
Semitism in France.*)[12]

---

11 Claudia Roth Pierpont, *Roth Unbound: A Writer and his Books* (New York: Farrar, Straus &
Giroux, 2014), p. 16.
12 "A Future for Andromaque" in *Legacies: Of Anti-Semitism in France* (Minneapolis: University
of Minnesota Press, 1983), pp. 34-63.

The inventiveness that has Giraudoux's last play offered up during World War II as the reverse-return of Racine's last play no doubt deserves to be characterized as the *invention* as much as (or even more than) the *discovery* of a key node in French cultural anti-Semitism. Whatever success I may have achieved in generalizing that gesture of restoring or inventing a lost anti-Semitic tradition in French letters might well raise a question (or an eyebrow) as to whether said anti-Semitism is more the "accomplishment" (or success) of the critic or reader than of the author (i.e., Giraudoux) himself. We have seen that perception surface in *The Ghost Writer* as the question asked by Nathan's mother: "Are you really anti-Semitic?" It is a perception that might be shared by Anthony Julius in his inquiry into the role a disastrous anti-Semitism can be regarded as playing in the aesthetic *success* of T.S. Eliot's poetry. And I take it that it is identical in tenor to the observation the psychoanalyst Jean Laplanche addressed to me upon reading my memoir *Adventures in the French Trade: Fragments Toward a Life.* In his words, during our last encounter, shortly before his death: "J'y ai bien reconnu tes amours anti-sémites…(I certainly recognized your anti-semitic loves)." Such would be the transposition as *schmutz* of the query (*as schmaltz*) of Nathan's mother.

The implication of Laplanche's remark is that any subject of fascination can be sustained only by a libidinal investment. And to the extent that French anti-semitism has been an ongoing subject of fascination for me, it is, at some level, a form of love… Whence, moreover, the interest of a second link between *The Ghost Writer* and Giraudoux, one involving the oscillation between Anne Frank declaring "I was a saint" and posthumously embracing that vocation, on the one hand, and an Anne Frank dreaming of her sensual or erotic existence and thinking of herself not as a Jew but as a full-blooded Dutch citizen. For that split in the psyche of Roth's Anne Frank is congruent with the split in the psyche of Giraudoux's Judith in the play of that name. The Giraudoux Judith falls in love with Holophernes, the Assyrian oppressor of her people, whom she was commissioned to seduce and decapitate. But if she slays him, it is not to protect her people under siege but in order to spare him the agony of knowing a decline after the perfection of the night they have spent together. She is not "Judith the saint," as she tells the rabbis who embrace her when she returns to the city with the head of Holophernes in hand, but "Judith the whore." She is, that is, the exemplar of *schmutz* not *schmaltz,* to use the Rothian distinction evoked above. And in an instance of repression or "testaments betrayed" (to use the titular phrase of Kundera's essay) it will be the defenders of *kitsch* or *schmaltz* who win out as the final curtain falls on Giraudoux's play.

In a certain context, of course, secularism itself can count as *schmutz*. Whence Anne's decision to betray her father in a letter to him that Roth (or his protagonist Zuckerman) qualifies as her "declaration of independence." The wish may be to become full-fledged Dutch, but the idiom is, of course, American. Which would entail ceasing to be a (Jewish) Frank and—why not?—becoming a (Dutch) "Franklin." Franklin, declaration of independence: we are reminded or seduced into believing that the posthumous Anne Frank(lin) is as...American in her fantasy as Nathan Zuckerman would be. Such is the "co-feeling" or "emotional telepathy," to use Kundera's terms, a configuration quite different from the identification that at times seems to bind Nathan Zuckerman and his fantasied love (to the extent that it can be distinguished from his love of fantasy).

From Judith and her "anti-Semitic love" to *The Madwoman of Chaillot* and her "eliminationist" designs on the Jews, by way of Laplanche's recognition of what he called my "anti-Semitic loves," we are ultimately confronted with the answer to Nathan's question: "Are you really anti-Semitic?"

**

Returning now from the Franco-American to the narrowly Viennese context in which Reitter exercises his mastery, we find the case of Stefan Zweig, whose version of *kitsch* amounted to what Kraus evoked as a certain "coziness" of the cultural monument, a decorative version of *Bildung* or culture as an "elevator that will lift you up to the loftiest heights." The case of Zweig as representative *schmoozer*, according to Kraus, as the world's most hated author (precisely because of his assimilationist aspiration to celebrity) is a reminder of the extent to which Kraus figures as his opposite number. For if Zweig over and again told the story of "genius as the triumph of individual agency," Kraus, by contrast, spoke of his own achievements as being "at bottom effects of structure." Ego to unconscious, then, as Zweig would be to Kraus. And ego, above all, would be a figure of *kitsch* as collective narcissism. Such would be the upshot of Kundera's reading of *kitsch*: "the need to gaze into the mirror of the beautifying lie and to be moved to tears of gratification at one's own reflection."

124

Reitter's investment in the idiosyncratic figure of Kraus, already evident in his monograph *The Anti-Journalist,* was even more striking in a collaboration with the novelist Jonathan Franzen published under the title *The Kraus Project.* The subject of that idiosyncratic work is the American Franzen's exhilarating but traumatic encounter abroad with the maddeningly opaque (or baroque) prose of Karl Kraus on Heine, both of them Jews, and the relation of the translation that ensued—not to mention the memoir, in the form of a commentary, it came to include—with diverse dimensions of the "Jewish question."

Now the strangeness of the scholar Reitter's work—as combined with that of the novelist—on Kraus is compounded for this reviewer by the uncanniness of the way in which the entire configuration seemed to mesh with a comparable experience he himself—i.e., I myself—had been subject to with the French psychoanalyst, Jacques Lacan. Or to phrase things in a manner congruent with Franzen-Reitter's experience with Karl Kraus, its focus is the maddeningly opaque (or baroque) prose of Lacan and the relation of the translation that ensued—not to mention the memoir, in the form of a commentary, it came to include—with diverse dimensions of the Jewish question.

The notion of a memoir in the form of a commentary on an author (Kraus) finds expression in such statements of Franzen (as abetted by Reitter) as: "Anger descended on me so near in time to when I fell in love with Kraus' writing that the two are practically indistinguishable." A comparable counterpoint between affect and textual configuration is featured in my *Adventures in the French Trade: Fragments Toward a Life,* which might at times appear to be (on the model of Franzen's effort, but preceding it) a kind of *Lacan Project* (which came to be known as *French Freud*). Its subtitle, *Structural Studies in Psychoanalysis,* seems, in fact, nicely adjusted to Kraus's insight, as reported by Reitter, that "his achievements were at bottom effects of structure."

Difficulty of style was of the essence. Scholem claimed provocatively that Kraus fought "a war for incomprehensibility." It is a perspective in harmony with Lacan's endorsements of reading Freud as though he were an author every bit as difficult—i.e., as incomprehensible—as Lacan himself. Indeed Kraus's promise to retract the whole of one of his essays should his adversary, H. Barr, understand a single sentence of it is well suited to Lacan's assault on ego psychology and its commonplaces.

And then there is the resonance between Léon Bloy as apocalyptician, self-described *démolisseur des idées reçues*, and principal predecessor, both stylistically and philosophically, of Lacan, on the one hand, and Kraus on Vienna as "research lab for world destruction," on the other. It is that insistence on disintegration *per se*, harbinger of a "death drive" redolent of Freud the thanatographer —beyond the fabled and well-documented intolerance of Kraus for psychoanalysis—which carries the day.

And then there is the relation to France and the French, as though the East European, in order to make his way through assimilation to the non-Jewish West, had to try harder, waxing still more western than mere entry into the province of German required. And waxing more western than German by definition entailed waxing French. Such would be the "linguistic overreach" of Jewish assimilationism, making the Jews—Heine, Kraus, Benjamin among others—the grand Francophiles of Germanic letters…

And thus it is, to choose a case close to home, that an American, the author of these pages, made his way eastward to the "source of sources," Paris, where he was to encounter "French Freud," the precipitate of a flow westward from Vienna of Jews whose vector was followed by another American, the novelist Franzen. It was a cultural configuration intuited retrospectively, and even resented on occasion in the pages of *The Kraus Project*. Including the following: "French literary theory did for mediocre American scholars what Kraus claims that Heine's Frenchified breeziness did for the journalistic hacks of Vienna." French, it was claimed by many a disillusioned Jew, had become "the most agreeable of excuses for avoiding literature itself." Derrida on Lacan on Edgar Allan Poe's "Purloined Letter" would not have put it differently.

What remained was a subjectivity split between the "stale pot pie of wit and woe" of Heine's *kitsch*, on the one hand, and the operettas of Offenbach, spoke-sung in all their vulgarity by Kraus, on the other. Transport to Paris the spectacle of Kraus holding forth in one of his Viennese concerts and one has the *séminaire* of Lacan. Such is the mobile stage, and such the apocalyptic backdrop, on and against which Franzen, with Reitter in tow, seems to have known a cultural change that defined him; and such as well was the stage on which this reader, arriving from the opposite extreme, was to know the change that turned him into what Hofmannsthal, as quoted by the genial Reitter, might have called a "solitary student of interconnectedness."

10

The End: Agamben on Auschwitz

The subject that brings us together, Holocaust denial or "revisionism," as it used to be called, strikes me as very much a chapter of French intellectual life of the 1980s, and one which it might have been thought (or hoped) had been put to rest (or exhausted) a generation ago.[1] But the motif of "alternative narratives," with its suggestion that the *bête immonde* of revisionism has perhaps been sophisticated back into existence, is intriguing, and it is that prospect, as it encroaches on the work of a prominent European intellectual, Giorgio Agamben, who is certainly *not* a Holocaust denier, that I will be considering in these remarks. Specifically, I will be focusing on what some have called his "most daring" book, but also perhaps "his most flawed" one, *Remnants of Auschwitz, Quel che resta di Auschwitz* (What Remains of Auschwitz) in the original Italian, which is significant since the book, which appeared in 1998, was followed in short order by an important reading of the Apostle Paul's Letter to the Corinthians titled *Il tempo che resta, The Time That Remains*.[2] The question of the relation between the remnants or remainders of Auschwitz and the time that remains (until the messianic end) is one that will occupy us later (if sufficient time remains). In any event, although it is hard not to be extremely critical of Agamben's little book, I will attempt—in the thought that my assignment is

---

1 A lecture at the Center for Holocaust and Genocide Studies at the University of Minnesota, April 13, 2011.
2 Leland de la Durantaye, Giorgio *Agamben: A Critical Introduction* (Stanford: Stanford University Press, 2009), p. 248.

not to tell the reader that a book he may not have read is not worth reading—to salvage a rather striking remnant from the book for you. I would not be averse to calling these remarks "What remains of *What remains of Auschwitz*."

Let me begin by offering some sort of context for the subject. Many will have a rough idea of Agamben's career less as a philosopher than as a particularly brilliant speculative philologist in the tradition of of Aby Warburg.[3] You may know of the awakening of his vocation as one of a very small contingent participating in Heidegger's seminar in the Provençal village of Le Thor in 1966. And you may be aware of the crucial role that Walter Benjamin, whom Agamben characterized as an "antidote" to Heidegger, has had for his thought.[4]

But the context I would offer at this point for understanding Agamben's book is less that of his multifaceted career—as literary critic, political theorist, religious thinker, and speculative philologist—than that of the subject of Holocaust denial or "revisionism" in French thought twenty years—i.e., a full generation—before he turned to the subject since it too impinges on his book. Not that I would offer an overview of the subject. I am, in fact, happy *not* to be an expert on Holocaust denial, and would probably distrust anyone who laid claim to such expertise. But I was involved in the debates over Holocaust revisionism in the 1980s and have a personal perspective that may prove useful.

Let me then divide the subject into two parts: a first instance that might be called transcendental revisionism; and a second instance that might be categorized as empiricist revisionism. The empiricist phase had to do with a diabolically clever and somewhat compulsive debunker of popular pieties, a professor of French literature named Robert Faurisson. It happens that I translated and prefaced the major French response to Faurisson, *Assassins of Memory*, by the distinguished French classicist and almost archetypal intellectual Pierre Vidal-Naquet.[5] The transcendental phase is more complicated and to the extent that it was amenable to some sort of revisionism it was certainly in spite of itself. I sometimes think of the conundrum at its core in terms of the paradoxical collision of an irresistible force and an unmovable object. The unmovable object will have been the genocide of the Jews, which was certainly the central moral

---

3 Ibid., p. XVIII.
4 "Agamben, le chercheur d'homme," *Libération* (Paris), April 1, 1999, pp. II-III.
5 Pierre Vidal-Naquet, *Assassins of Memory: Essays on the Denial of the Holocaust*, translated and with a foreword by Jeffrey Mehlman (New York: Columbia University Press, 1992).

reference for my generation. The irresistible force was the most potent discourse available to my generation, a discourse notoriously corrosive of the categories of *reference* and *centrality*. What happened at their intersection will be our focus in a moment.

But let us turn first to Vidal-Naquet's *Assassins of Memory* and what I have called the empiricist instance. On December 29, 1978, Robert Faurisson, a literature professor who had first come to popular attention with an effort to demystify the reputation of Lautréamont, adopted the tone of the skeptical anti-Nazi, in an article in *Le Monde* titled "The Problem of the Gas Chambers or the Rumor of Auschwitz." "The Rumor of Auschwitz" was a reference to a notorious anti-Semitic rumor known as the Rumor of Orléans.[6] Faurisson's point was that the Jews had been slandered in Orléans and now the Germans were being slandered worldwide. The gas chambers were a technical impossibility, he claimed; those operating them would have killed themselves in the process; the deaths at Auschwitz were numerous, but caused by typhus; if the place was known as *anus mundi*, it was because of the diarrhea. The war was over; happily Hitler had lost; it was time now to do away with the propagandistic lie of a genocide, based as it was on the technical impossibility of the installations at Auschwitz having served as gas chambers.

Vidal-Naquet, outraged, ended up publishing an entire book against Faurisson and his supporters, many of whom were on the left, based on the principle that one does not stoop to debate with someone so sadistically perverse as to deny the Nazi genocide of the Jews. Which is to say that the book itself, despite being well received on the cover of the New York Times Book Review when it appeared, was a disappointment.[7] At least such is my perception. Were a demonstration needed I would simply say that the concluding two pages consisted of the lyrics of the cynical Argentine tango *Cambalache*: the world had indeed become a junk shop (*Cambalache*), Vidal-Naquet seemed to be saying, if a professor could get away with purveying the kind of nonsense that Faurisson was spewing suavely forth…

The foreword I wrote to the volume was marked by its melancholy. *Révisionniste* had been the word used for the champions of Dreyfus during the eponymous Affair. The Vidal-Naquet clan had been a great *révisionniste* fam-

---

6 See Edgar Morin, *La Rumeur d'Orléans* (Paris: Seuil, 1969).
7 Walter Reich, "Erasing the Holocaust" in the New York Times, July 11, 1993.

ily. Now here was their scion refusing to debate, defending what his adversary, given that refusal to debate, had no trouble characterizing as a dogma. Vidal-Naquet was even doing battle with Noam Chomsky, who had chimed in with a defense of free speech that ended up being used as a preface to a Faurisson publication.[8] "Truth on the March," Zola's celebrated slogan during the Affair, was adopted by Faurisson. Small wonder that Vidal-Naquet could find no better words with which to conclude his book than the cynical lyrics of a tango.

Finally, Vidal-Naquet appealed to the scholarship of his friend the Princeton historian, Arno Mayer, whose history of the genocide, once it appeared, he suggested, would definitively reduce the revisionist camp to silence. Or so he hoped. Mayer's controversial book, when it appeared, insisted that "sources for the study of the gas chambers are at once rare and unreliable."[9] Faurisson was jubilant and Vidal-Naquet, I assume, depressed.

Now the one valuable result of the Faurisson affair, and one that will bear on our understanding of Agamben, concerns the support Faurisson received from the far left (and in particular the group, "La Vieille Taupe"). Alain Finkielkraut convincingly argued that at issue was doing away with any possibility of distinguishing between capitalist regimes of greater and lesser evil.[10] If the gas chambers did not exist, the Americans, from the point of view of partisans of the class struggle, were no better than the Germans. And so it became possible to wish—or spuriously argue—them (i.e., the gas chambers) out of existence.

Let me turn now to what I have called the transcendental wing of the revisionist question. If deconstruction was hell-bent on dismantling the very categories of reference and centrality, what might it have to say about the central moral reference of an entire generation? For a long time, the answer appeared to be nothing. Derrida, who was, of course, not a revisionist, for a long time preferred to go no where near the genocide of the Jews. Blanchot's

---

8 Noam Chomsky, "Some Elementary Comments on the Rights of Freedom of Expression," reproduced as a preface to R. Faurisson, *Mémoire en défense contre ceux qui m'accusent de falsifier l'histoire* (Paris: La Vieille Taupe, 1980).
9 Arno J. Mayer, *Why Did the Heavens Not Darken: The "Final Solution"* in History (New York: Pantheon, 1988), p. XVIII.
10 Alain Finkielkraut, *L'Avenir d'une negation: Réflexion sur la question du genocide* (Paris: Seuil, 1982), pp. 15-58.

anti-Jewish writings of the 1930s, about which he knew, he never mentioned.[11] Paul de Man's notorious anti-Semitic article during the war in *Le Soir* posed a real problem, but Derrida finessed it by interpreting de Man's phrase "vulgar anti-Semitism" rather unconvincingly not as a vulgar trend within anti-Semitism but as anti-Semitism being inherently and essentially vulgar in itself.[12]

The closest Derrida came, I believe, to the Holocaust during the 1980s, was his rather brilliant little book on the category of Mind (or *Geist*), *De l'esprit*, in Heidegger.[13] The argument is that Heidegger, in 1927, consolidates his discovery (of an authentic interrogation of the being of *Dasein*) by relegating Mind, *Geist*, to the category of those all too Cartesian words that he would have us use only in quotation marks. Whereupon Heidegger becomes a Nazi and drops the quotation marks—i.e., he becomes a humanist of sorts, with a real investment in *Geist* or Mind. Finally, in 1953, in pages on the poet Georg Trakl, the repressed returns in the form of a *Geist* derivative not from Plato (and *geistig*) but from old-Germanic *geistlich*, indicating a metaphorical fire. Derrida lets us know that the old-Germanic is part of a "brutal foreclosure" of the Hebrew *ruach, spirit, wind*...[14] Moreover he goes to special lengths to translate the German *entsetzt* in the Trakl poem not as *déplace*, but as *déporte*. Put it all together—Nazism, fire, exclusion of the Hebrew, deportation, all of them metaphorical—and one has the metaphorical matrix of the Holocaust, with an implicit warning not to take it literally (Heidegger's error in 1934, when he dropped the quotation marks). This is as close to a deconstruction of the Holocaust as Derrida, I submit, ever came.[15]

Having evoked both the empirical wing and the transcendental wing (in spite of itself) of 1980s revisionism, we would, at this point, move a generation ahead to Agamben's *Remnants of Auschwitz*. The circumstances around the

---

11 Cf. Derrida, Parages (Paris: Galilée, 1986). See, however, Derrida's *Demeure: Maurice Blanchot* (Paris: Galilée, 1998), its comments on Blanchot's *L'Instant de ma mort* (Paris: Fata Morgana, 1994), and my remarks on those comments in Chapter I of this volume.

12 Cf. Derrida, "Like the Sound of the Sea Deep Within a Shell: Paul de Man's War" in *Critical Inquiry*, Spring 1988.

13 Derrida, *De l'esprit: Heidegger et la question* (Paris: Galilée, 1987).

14 Ibid., p. 165.

15 See "Perspectives: On Paul de Man and *Le Soir* in J. Mehlman, *Genealogies of the Text: Literature, Psychoanalysis, and Politics in Modern France* (Cambridge, Cambridge University Press, 1995), pp. 125-128.

text are particularly auspicious. It is translated into French by Pierre Alféri, who happens to be Derrida's son.[16] In English the translator is the brilliant Daniel Heller-Roazen of Princeton, son of the eminent historian of psychoanalysis, Paul Roazen.[17] The book is the object of a full length critique by Philippe Mesnard, the author of a polemical work targeting Blanchot's right-wing journalism in the 1930s.[18] Plainly, it occurred to me, here was a text I was slated to attend to—which is what I now will do.

Agamben's point of departure, already prepared for in the series that began with *Homo Sacer*, a series of which the Auschwitz volume is the third, is the notion that the camp, the concentration camp, is the paradigmatic institution of modern times, or in the author's words: "the hidden paradigm of the political space of modernity."[19] The reader will immediately recognize Michel Foucault's notion of the prison, the architectural arrangement of Bentham's all-seeing Panopticon, as the exemplary modern institution.[20] And Agamben, in fact, suggests that his work is a prolongation of Foucault's—from prison to camp. For those who may have found the exclusionary realm of the prison already too *exceptional* or marginal a space to be promoted to centrality in our normalized world, who may, for instance, have preferred the school (as in Ivan Illich's *Deschooling Society*, which was roughly contemporary with Foucault's book) as paradigm, the choice of the camp for such exemplarity comes as a shock indeed.[21] (One would need all the parodic and lyrical wit of the authors of the musical *Urinetown*, that neo-Weillian masterpiece for post-revolutionary times, to pull it off, and even then only half-seriously. Recall the exchange. Young Jimmy, about to be thrown off a roof: "You mean Urinetown is death?" To which Mr. Gladwell, warden of the camp, replies: "Well, that's one inter-

---

16 *Ce qui reste d'Auschwitz*, trans. P. Alféri (Paris: Rivages, 2003).

17 *Remnants of Auschwitz: The Witness and the Archive*, trans. D. Heller-Roazen (New York: Zone Books, 2002).

18 Philippe Mesnard and Claudine Kahan, *Giorgio Agamben à l'épreuve d'Auschwitz* (Paris: Kimé, 2001). On Blanchot, cf. Philippe Mesnard, *Maurice Blanchot, le sujet de l'engagement* (Paris: l'Harmattan, 1996).

19 Agamben, *Homo Sacer: Sovereign Power and Bare Life*, trans. D. Heller-Roazen (Stanford: Stanford University Press, 1998), p. 123.

20 Cf. M. Foucault, *Surveiller et punir: Naissance de la prison* (Paris: Gallimard, 1975).

21 Cf. Ivan Illich, *Deschooling Society* (New York: Harper & Row, 1971).

pretation...")[22] The choice of exacerbating, in all seriousness, Foucault's prison into a concentration camp, of course, may even strike us as sensationalistic. As though the vanguard thought of the 1970s—Foucault, in this case—were in need of a new emotional rush in order to command the attention of a new and slightly jaded generation of readers.

Or perhaps, in search of the motivation behind Agamben's construct, one should above all recall the imperative of a (long deferred) rendez-vous implicit in every discourse pretending to pre-eminence—again, Foucault, in this case—with what all were prepared to treat as the pre-eminent event of the twentieth century—the genocide of the Jews, in this case. We won't know the ultimate value of a discourse, as it were, until we hear what it has to say about the Holocaust.

To this mix, we should add mention of the tutelary role of Carl Schmitt in Agamben's thought, the notion that the rule or norm was best understood as a function—or even as an after-effect—of the exception.[23] Thus for Derrida speech, the linguistic norm, was said to be a mirage generated by an exacerbation of a skewed version of writing, the exception. Even as, for Foucault, as already suggested, the exclusionary space of the Panopticon would be said to lie at the center of our institutions. Translate into the idiom of Agamben's *Remnants of Auschwitz*, "the extreme [or exceptional] situation becomes the very paradigm of modern life."[24]

Let us consider a version of this omnipresence of Auschwitz. Agamben quotes Primo Levi (who himself is drawing on the writing of Mikos Nyszli a Hungarian-Jewish physician assigned to the *Sonderkommando*, the accursed crew—of Jews—whose task was to assist in the killing). During a period of respite from their grueling work, a soccer match is improvised between the SS and members of the *Sonderkommando*. Levi comments: "Other members of the SS and the rest of the squad are present at the game; they take sides, bet, applaud, urge the players on as if, rather than at the gates of hell, the game were

---

22 Mark Hollman & Greg Kotis, *Urinetown* (London: Faber & Faber, 2003). The dystopian conceit of the musical is that at a time of severe drought, all those who fail to pay a fee "for the privilege to pee" are carted off to an ill-defined "urinetown."
23 See in particular Giorgio Agamben, *State of Exception*, trans. Kevin Attell (Chicago: University pf Chicago Press, 2005), pp. 3-31.
24 *Remnants of Auschwitz*, p. 49.

taking place on the village green."[25] Agamben characterizes that moment of apparent normalcy as "the true horror of the camp. … For that match is never over; it continues as if interrupted. It is the perfect and eternal cipher of the 'gray zone,' which knows no time and is in every place."[26]

That soccer match, as evoked by Agamben (via Levi), provokes several thoughts:

1. In this passage, as in much of his book, Agamben comes across as a latter-day Dante whose Virgil, through the twentieth century hell of Auschwitz, is Primo Levi. And one thinks: How odd that the vanguard discourse of France in the 1970s—Foucault, but much more than Foucault, as we shall soon see—should by the end of the century be recast as part of a scenario that sees two Italians acting out the Inferno of Dante…

2. The soccer match in the death camp functions as a restricted economy, almost a mirage, within the general economy of the extermination. But consider the terms in which Agamben evokes it: it "knows no time and is in every place." "[The match] repeats itself in every match in our stadiums, in every television broadcast, in the normalcy of everyday life."[27] One could readily imagine such a perception as the symptom of a survivor who projects the terms of his trauma everywhere. But this is not Levi the survivor but Agamben the theorist who is speaking, and his statement seems part mystical vision, part polemic against historical research, reduced to its most positivistic and banal. "The aporia of Auschwitz is, indeed, the very aporia of historical knowledge: a non-coincidence between facts and truth, between verification and comprehension."[28]

3. Note, moreover, that once Auschwitz is said to be everywhere ("every match in our stadiums, every television broadcast"), its uniqueness—its extraordinariness—has been decisively eroded. Once it is there in the "normalcy of our everyday life," has it not been reduced to something almost normal?

---

25 Ibid., p.25.
26 Ibid., p. 26.
27 Ibid., p. 26.
28 Ibid., p. 12.

4. We may already intuit the arc of Agamben's argument. Heidegger the sometime Nazi was to be counteracted by the messianic Benjamin, said to be his "antidote"—an agent of *euporia* (or hope) to counter the aporia encountered in Heidegger. But all transpires as though what lay await in Benjamin for Agamben was above all the presence of Carl Schmitt, theorist of the state-of-exception (that gave us camps in the first place) and crown jurist of the Third Reich. We know that Benjamin had mentioned Schmitt in a *curriculum vitae* as a principal inspiration of his work on *Trauerspiel.* And in December 1930, he wrote to Schmitt that he hoped to do for the philosophy of art what Schmitt, in his book on dictatorship, had done for the philosophy of the State.[29] There is a component of Benjamin's thought, that is, which could lead a reader (*du côté de chez Carl Schmitt*) still deeper into the nightmare of the twentieth century and such appears to be the case of Agamben in his book on Auschwitz.

Now the condition of Agamben's generalization of Auschwitz to "paradigmatic" status is a relegation of the gas chambers to secondary importance. We have already seen how such denial of the gas chambers figured as part of the ideological arsenal of a fragment of the far-left in the 1980s: no gas chambers meant no *essential* difference between the two capitalist regimes—Germany and the United States—locked in conflict in a Second World War. Agamben, who is in no way a Holocaust denier, is nonetheless sufficiently of the far-left to want to demote the gas chambers, the principal vehicle of the genocide, to secondary status, and he does so through the crucial maneuver of promoting the figure of the *Muselmann* to central importance.

The *Muselmann*, we know, was a dreaded figure of near autistic apathy, physically and mentally wasted, a kind of "staggering corpse," one of the living dead," a person who inspired no sympathy in his fellow inmates since he had lost all dignity and no longer offered any resistance to the brutality around him. In Levi's terms, he was one of the "drowned," someone who had "touched bottom." When Bruno Bettelheim founded his Orthogenic School in Chicago to treat autistic children, it was conceived of as a kind of counter-camp in which children demonstrating many of the symptoms of *Muselmänner* were to be rehabilitated.[30]

---

29 Cited in Jacob Taubes, *En divergent accord: A propos de Carl Schmitt,* trans. Philippe Ivernel (Paris: Rivages, 2003), p. 52.
30 *Remnants of Auschwitz,* p. 46.

There is debate about the origin of the term. The principal consensus is that the name was used for the particularly wretched denizens of the camp because Moslems were thought to "submit unconditionally" to the will of God.[31] That state of utter submissiveness, a complete loss of dignity or independence, was said to characterize the camp's "Moslems." It has also been suggested that because they were autistically closed in on themselves, they were "like mussel-men."[32]

What is most significant is that theirs was an experience of near-collapse as a result of starvation and disease. At one level, it made no sense to kill them since they were virtually dead already. The horror they inspired, that is, was quite different from that associated with the shock of wealthy bourgeois who were suddenly "selected" for the gas chamber upon arrival at the camp. But if the *Muselmänner*, the camp zombies, were to replace the gas chambers at the center of our iconography—and thus of our understanding—of the camps, Agamben, who was anything but a "revisionist" or "denier," would have taken a crucial step in the direction of those far-left advocates of Holocaust denial. He would, after all, eventually be capable of comparing the (no doubt) listless detainees of Guantanamo to "the Jews in the Nazi *Lager*," a move that could only be justified (*et encore*!) if one decided to bracket the gas chambers or reduce them to subsidiary importance.[33]

Now there is a central paradox, according to Agamben, affecting the situation of the *Muselmann*. On the one hand, he is the person who has experienced the camp at its worst—and is thus the "complete witness."[34] On the other, his state of near autistic degradation, that state of "no return" into which, according to Bettelheim, he had descended, made him the least trustworthy of speakers. He is essentially speechless. But if such be the case, then the only witness is disqualified, through a kind of epistemological hitch, on logical grounds. In Agamben's words: "Let us, indeed posit Auschwitz, that to which it is not possible to bear witness; and let us also posit the *Muselmann* as the absolute impossibility of bearing witness…"[35] Has a memorialist of the genocide ever come closer to the position of a Holocaust denier.

---

31 Ibid., p. 45.
32 Mesnard and Kahan, p. 43.
33 Agamben, *State of Exception*, p. 4.
34 *Remnants of Auschwitz*, p. 47.
35 Ibid., p. 164.

Agamben's paradox calls for several comments:

1. First, and quite empirically, it is not the case that the *Muselmänner* did not bear witness. At the very end of his book, Agamben, out of intellectual honesty (or perhaps love of paradox), offers a small anthology of statements by former *Muselmänner*. From which I select a single example, the words of Feliksa Piekarska: "I was a *Muselmann* for a short while. I remember that after the move to the barrack, I completely collapsed as far as my psychological life was concerned. The collapse took the following form: I was overcome by a general apathy; nothing interested me; I no longer reacted to either external or internal stimuli; I stopped washing, even when there was water; I no longer even felt hungry…"[36] Such was the extreme depression of those who were said to wander through the camp "like stray dogs."[37]

2. Secondly, removing the focus from the gas chambers and those who manned them curiously deflects attention from those who may have been the principal archivists of the camp, the *Sonderkommando*. The point has been well registered by Philippe Mesnard and Claudine Kahan. The members of the *Sonderkommando* led the strangest of embittered lives. On the one hand, manning the gas chambers and crematoria, they were engaged in the most grueling and dehumanizing of jobs. On the other, because they were in almost immediate contact with those arriving at the camp from outside, and who would be immediately exterminated, they had greater access than any other category of deportee to goods arriving from outside the camp: alcohol, cigarettes, underwear, etc. Theirs was an existence split, maddeningly, between toil amidst the corpses, and what comparatively passed for a measure of luxury among those in the camp. This resulted in incredible bitterness, but also in sufficient vigor to sustain a burning desire to bear witness. The result was, among other testimony, the scrolls of the *Sonderkommando* that were buried near the crematoria and the burial ditches and were known as the Meguilès Auschwitz. The authors include Haim Herman, Lejb Langfus, Zalman Gradowski, and Marcel Nadsari, among others.[38] Their purpose, as the issue of YIVO Bleter that gathered a number of

---

36 Ibid., p. 166.
37 Ibid., p. 167.
38 Mesnard and Kahan, pp. 19-20.

their texts at the end of the war, claimed, was "to create a tableau of how life was "lived"—as opposed to terminated—at Auschwitz. What a normal day there was like […] Our writing should not be weighed on a literary scale. But we have much to tell, even if literarily, we stammer. We will relate things as we can, in our language."[39] But these texts, central testimony on Auschwitz, are overlooked by Agamben, fascinated as he is with the *Muselmann* and the essential "lacuna" affecting the testimony he might be expected to offer.

Here then is an empiricist disqualification of evidence of life—and death—in Auschwitz. The *Meguiles Auschwitz*, the testimony of members of the *Sonderkommando*, are largely overlooked by Agamben and the "complete witness," the *Muselmann*, is shown, on logical grounds, to be essentially flawed. But, as in the revisionism of the 1980s, Agamben's considerations of Auschwitz also bear a transcendental burden, to which we now shall turn. For Agamben, from the outset, appears to have been concerned as much with the future of vanguard French thought as with the truth of Auschwitz.

The challenge for him lay in finding a theoretical coefficient to articulate with the paradox inherent in the discursive situation of the *Muselmann*, what I have called the "hitch" in the "complete" witness's voice. Agamben finds this coefficient in the linguistics (or discourse analysis) of Emile Benveniste, and specifically in what he imagines to be their transition to the kind of political history of speech acts associated with Michel Foucault. Benveniste's celebrated analysis deals with the fact that subjectivity is a function of the entirely performative role of interlocutory pronouns—and other so-called "shifters"—and the toll they take on the presumed constative function of linguistic signs. Ego exists because ego, in conversation, says "I," but "I" (in conversation) will change its (constative) meaning, the person to whom it refers, depending on which party to the conversation is uttering it. It all proceeds as though the categories of *énonciation*, the performative instance, and *énoncé*, the constative, formed a zero-sum game. The more valid the *énonciation*, the anchoring of the subject in discourse, the less valid, Agamben seems to be speculating, the *énoncé*. Pressed to the limit, the analysis yields the following conclusion, italicized by Agamben: *"The subject of enunciation is composed of discourse and exists in discourse alone. But, for this very reason, once the subject is in discourse, he can say nothing; he cannot speak."*[40]

---

39 Ibid., p. 21.
40 *Remnants of Auschwitz*, p. 117.

Agamben would appear to be weaving a complex metaphor or analogy between a historical reality (the debilitating hitch in the "impossible" testimony of the "complete witness," the *Muselmann*), on the one hand, and the theory of subjectivity in language of Benveniste, on the other (the price that the constative, reference, appears to be required to pay for every achievement of the performative). What the one has to do with the other is a problem of considerable scope that Agamben comes nowhere close to solving. One attempt on his part consists in assigning the emotion of shame, frequently said to be the specific sentiment of survivors of the genocide, to the tension (between performative and constative) that Agamben unearthed as a linguistic universal in Benveniste. "Shame," he ends up saying with a certain vagueness, "is truly something like the hidden structure of all subjectivity and consciousness."[41]

If that doesn't convince you, Agamben offers up one last attempt to join the two terms of the complex metaphor, to turn them into something more than a vague analogy. "One evening in 1969," we are told, "Emile Benveniste [...] suffered a stroke on a street in Paris. Without identification papers, he was not recognized. By the time he was identified, he had already suffered a complete and incurable aphasia that lasted until his death in 1972."[42] Benveniste, Agamben tells us, was on the verge of making a major advance, "a metasemantics built on a semantics of enunciation," when his career was brutally cut short. It was left to Michel Foucault to "perfectly realize" the discipline that Benveniste had glimpsed before his collapse.[43] In sum, it is as though Benveniste, having intuited the (Foucaultian) core of Agamben's theory of –or metaphor for—Auschwitz, was turned into a *Muselmann*, rendered tragically mute for the rest of his days. And French thought seemed to show up at its most eminent in order to bemoan or celebrate the event: Foucault, in his theory of the archive: "the dark margin encircling and limiting every act of speech," was there to pick up the slack and pursue the project Benveniste had only glimpsed.[44] And Derrida was even summoned to attend, if only to be put in his place. In Agamben's words: "The intimacy that betrays our non-coincidence with ourselves is the place of testimony. *Testimony takes place in the non-place of articulation.* In the

41 Ibid., p. 128.
42 Ibid., p. 137.
43 Ibid., p. 139.
44 Ibid., p. 144.

non-place of the Voice stands not writing, but the witness"—i.e., the impossible witness, the *Muselmann*.[45]

**

It is time to save a remnant from the *Remnants of Auschwitz*, a book, it will be seen, whose arbitrariness is in many ways staggering. As I said, I did not come here to urge you not to read a book many of you will not have read. Consider then the following passage:

> The space of the camp [...] can even be represented as a series of concentric circles that, like waves, incessantly wash up against a central non-place, where the *Muselmann* lives. [...] The entire population of the camp is, indeed, nothing other than an immense whirlpool obsessively spinning around a faceless center. But like the mystical rose of Dante's Paradiso, this anonymous vortex is "painted in our image" (*pinta della nostra effige*); it bears the true likeness of man.[46]

Here then is the *Muselmann* at the center of a mystical vision. We had earlier talked of the strangeness of French vanguard thought staging what may be regarded as a last hurrah under the auspices of two Italians acting out Dante: Primo Levi as Virgil, Giorgio Agamben as Dante, making their way through the Hell of Auschwitz. Here though we have been removed to Paradiso, a presumed salvation, although one centered on the arch-melancholic, almost Satanic figure of the *Muselmann*. Earlier we had also quoted Agamben on the shape of his career: from Heidegger to the presumed "antidote," Walter Benjamin, Agamben's presumed ticket from *aporia* to *euporia*, indeed the euphoria of salvation. And we had noted the cruel irony that saw Agamben encounter in Benjamin above all the work of Carl Schmitt, theorist of the "state of exception" and crown jurist of the Third Reich. Auschwitz, he would have us believe, was everywhere.

---

45 Ibid., p. 130.
46 Ibid., pp. 51-52.

There is, however, a very different inspiration in Benjamin, very much in opposition to Schmitt, namely that of Gershom Scholem. Surely, the reference to the remnant as an inherently "theologico-messianic concept" at the end of *Remnants of Auschwitz* justifies a glance *du côté de chez Scholem*, so to speak.[47] Moreover, the fact that Agamben would dedicate his subsequent book—on the Apostle Paul—to another thinker, another would-be heir to Benjamin, whose allegiances seemed similarly divided between Scholem and Schmitt, namely Jacob Taubes, offers us further encouragement.[48] What follows is a masque or a *Trauerspiel* of sorts, the staging of an effort to redeem Agamben's book and to fight the good fight against Scholem's apparent adversary, Schmitt, in the struggle for Benjamin's soul. The backdrop, elaborately designed in the manner of the baroque masque, offers a view of Agamben's Hell, Auschwitz, at the center of whose "concentric circles" we find an almost allegorical figure of Satanic melancholy, the *Muselmann*, mystically transformed in Agamben's telling into a salvific figure of hope, Dante's *rosa mystica*. Foucault, Benveniste (in a state of paralysis), and Derrida are in attendance. The curtain is about to rise.

The action is largely in the form of a conversation that actually occurred at the Café du Dôme in Montparnasse, 1927.[49] Scholem imparts to Benjamin, in a febrile state, the thrust of the discovery he has just made in Oxford, the existence of a full-blown antonimian theology within Judaism. Everything begins with Sabbatai Zevi, the legendary false Messiah, a seemingly familiar story. In 1665, stricken with migraine headaches, Sabbatai Zevi, a mediocrity living in Smyrna, Turkey, heads off to the Holy Land to consult with Nathan of Gaza, an illuminate, in search of a cure. Nathan takes one look at him and announces that the previous night he had dreamt the coming of the Messiah and he had Sabbatai Zevi's face. Whereupon he tells Sabbatai Zevi that he is not ill; he is the messiah. In short order, a decision is taken to bring the good news to the rest of Jewry, which meant taking the fledgling messiah on the road. The Jews of Europe, in their suffering, were prepared for a messiah and welcomed him enthusiastically.

---

47 Ibid., p. 162.

48 On the Taubes-Benjamin relation (by way of the Scholem-Schmitt tension), see J. Mehlman, "De la pédagogie abusive: malaise dans la transmission" in *Avec George Steiner: Les chemins de la culture* (Paris: Albin Michel, 2010), pp. 87-100.

49 Gershom Scholem, *Walter Benjamin: The Story of a Friendship*, trans. Harry Zohn (New York: Schocken, 1981), p. 136.

And then the collapse came. The Ottoman Sultan, vexed by the power accruing to the "King of the Jews," summoned him to Istanbul and confronted him with a rather austere choice: conversion to Islam or death. Sabbatai Zevi opted for conversion and the official story came to a close.

At this point Gershom Scholem intervenes to demonstrate that a considerable number of Jews never, in fact, abandoned their apostate messiah. Instead, a new subterranean theology emerged based on the proposition that at this point in the redemptive process, the messiah was obliged to enter into evil in order to defeat it from within. And his disciples were ordered to follow suit. The Law was to be fulfilled by violating it. Antinomianism was to be the order of the day.[50]

Eventually, according to Scholem, after generations of violating the Law, the mystical-heretical reasons for doing so were quite simply forgotten. A new justification for not obeying the law was invented. It was called Enlightenment, which was thus, in Scholem's inspired reading, no more than the precipitate of a decrepit mystical heresy no longer aware of its own existence.

But what is the relation of all this to Agamben's book about Auschwitz, the action of our Trauerspiel-masque to its backdrop? Quite simply that Agamben's vision, centered as it is on a Dante-inspired image of salvation (*Paradiso*) embodied by the *Muselmann* messiah, seems almost a rebus of Scholem's argument. It is almost as though Agamben, in his desire to repeat the existence of Benjamin, had substituted an icon of Sabbatai Zevi, the pathologically gloomy Muslim messiah of the Jews, a man of Satanic disposition, for Benjamin's talismanic Angel (Angelus Novus) as painted by Klee. For it should not be forgotten that Benjamin's secret name, Agesilaus Santander, as Scholem explained, was an anagram of Der Angelus Satanas, the angel Satan—seated at the center of Hell.[51] It was that melancholic Angel, as painted by Paul Klee, now become the "angel of history," who would show up at the outset of the Second World War, taking in the "one single catastrophe that keeps piling wreckage on wreckage," in the Ninth Thesis on the Philosophy of History.

Or perhaps we should see the Muselmann messiah at the center of

---

50 Gershom Scholem, "Redemption Through Sin" in *The Messianic Idea in Judaism* (New York: Schocken, 1971), pp. 78-141.

51 See Scholem, "Walter Benjamin and His Angel" in Scholem, *On Jews and Judaism in Crisis*, ed. W. Dannhauser (New York: Schocken, 1976), pp. 198-236.

Agamben's vision of Auschwitz, in its relation to the conversation in Paris about the apostate (and thus) Muslim messiah, Sabbatai Zevi, in terms of what Benjamin called a "dialectical image": a kind of "picture puzzle" or constellation that brings the dialectic of history to a standstill and shocks or rips its way out of what seemed to be a continuum.[52] The emergent "now-time" as Benjamin calls it, or the *kairos*, to use Agamben's term, is charged with "splinters of the messianic," according to Benjamin. In Agamben's book on Auschwitz, those splinters are the fragments of Rilke and Keats on shame that Agamben would have bear witness to the horror of events they, of course, never witnessed. One is tempted to match up the passages from Rilke and Keats in Agamben with others from Baudelaire in Benjamin. The match is perfect and the function the same.[53] One could continue constructing the Benjamin-Agamben constellation, within the space opened by our two "Muslim—or Muselmann—messiahs": Agamben's insistence that our ethical categories are fundamentally "contaminated" by legal categories and Paul's polemic against the Law in Agamben's *The Time That Remains*; the insistence of Jacob Taubes, Agamben's dedicatee for that book, that the best guide to understanding the Apostle Paul is the chapter of Scholem's *Major Trends in Jewish Mysticism*, a book dedicated to Benjamin, whose focus is Sabbatianism…

At bottom, then, Agamben's book on Auschwitz takes him farther and farther from Auschwitz and deeper and deeper into Benjamin and the battle for his soul between Scholem and Schmitt that we have attempted to stage. It would be tempting to elaborate this, but, as our would-be messiahs have been known to put it, "the time that remains," *il tempo che resta*, is scant.

---

52 Richard Wolin, *Walter Benjamin: An Aesthetic of Redemption* (New York: Columbia University Press, 1982), p. 125.

53 Compare, for instance, the outcast-beggars Agamben cites from Rilke's *Notebooks of Malte Laurids Brigge*, "husks of men that fate has spewed out" (p. 61), and Baudelaire's "vieux saltimbanque" in *Le Spleen de Paris*. Rilke: "They know that I am one of them." Baudelaire: "I have just seen the image of the old man of letters who has survived the generation whose brilliant entertainer he once was."

Postscript

Shortly before her death, during a visit I made to New York to see her (and illiterate though she was in all but the Yiddish of her daily paper), my maternal grandmother was stunned to discover a vintage photograph on the cover of a volume of Proust I happened to be carrying with me. Why, she asked, are you walking around with a photo of my husband? I had never known my grandfather, who died in New York in the 1920s. The incident, moreover, elicited little more than a fleeting smile—until, years later, well into the current century, I stumbled upon a photo of my grandfather, Nathan Melnikoff. The acute resemblance between the two photos was unmistakable, issuing in what

I am inclined to think of as a call to superimposition of near identical images.

Between those two episodes, I had studied in Aix-en-Provence with Charles Mauron, high priest of a cult of textual superimposition. He was, among other things, Bloomsbury's favorite Frenchman, much admired by Virginia Woolf and dedicatee of E. M. Forster's classic Aspects of the Novel. He also served as mayor of Saint-Rémy de Provence and was eventually tapped for the renaming of the street currently known as the Avenue Charles Mauron. The episodes just listed span a full five generations—from my grandmother mistaking a portrait of Proust for that of her late husband to a visit to Saint-Rémy and a snapshot of two of my grandchildren and their parents on the Avenue Charles Mauron.

Five generations, then—from grandparent to grandchild (and then said grandchild to his or her grandchildren), yielding a tabernacle, a trellis of newly read texts, sustenance for the (writing) reader I continue to be…

www.ingramcontent.com/pod-product-compliance
Lightning Source LLC
Chambersburg PA
CBHW060234030426
42335CB00014B/1453